10
minute

GW00801808

Maths
Assessments

for ages 9-10

CONTENTS

Assessment for learning

It is widely acknowledged that effective learning takes place where teachers understand their pupils' standards of achievement and lead the pupils forwards from these standards.

> Assessment for learning is the process of seeking and interpreting evidence for use by learners and their teachers to decide where the learners are in their learning, where they need to go and how best to get there.
>
> (Assessment for Learning: 10 principles – Assessment Reform Group)

This book will help you to assess your pupils' progress by providing activities that are quick and easy to administer, that can be used on a regular basis and that will help you build a profile of each pupil's attainment. Each activity will provide you with evidence of achievement that you can use for on-going pupil assessment and will help you focus your teaching and planning on the specific learning requirements of each child in your class.

Using the materials in this book will provide opportunities for both formative and summative assessment. It is recommended that the activities are used on a regular basis as part of an ordinary maths lesson, for continuous formative assessment. Recording the progress of each pupil, using the recording grid provided, will also assist you in making regular summative assessments in relation to National Curriculum levels of attainment.

All aspects of the *Framework for mathematics* for Year 5 are addressed through the assessment of separate learning objectives. These learning objectives are drawn from Strands 2 to 7 of the Framework:

2. Counting and understanding number
3. Knowing and using number facts
4. Calculating
5. Understanding shape
6. Measuring
7. Handling data

Many of the activities can also be used to support your assessment of Strand 1 (*Using and applying mathematics*). The teachers' notes accompanying each activity indicate where an assessment is particularly relevant to this.

How to use the activities for assessing pupils' progress

Ideally, pupils will work with an adult on an individual basis or in a very small group to enable the adult to make effective judgements about each individual's achievement. Everything achieved by the pupil should be a learning experience, perhaps where a particular skill or an aspect of knowledge is being strengthened and consolidated, or where a style of layout or method is being encountered for the first time. However, the assessment activities should only be used when the pupil has some prior experience of the work being assessed.

A pupil may be able to complete some, but not all, of the learning objectives. Any adult working closely with a pupil may discover 'gaps' in their understanding that can be reported back to the class teacher for monitoring and planning purposes. Further practice, focusing on specific areas, will help to fill these gaps and the assessment can then be repeated when the pupil is ready.

What's on the CD

The CD that accompanies this book can be used on a computer or CD player and features an audio track that can be used for the assessments that require audio. Children are often more focused when listening to a recording as the sound of a different voice helps to hold their attention. The teachers' notes for each assessment indicate whether there is an accompanying audio track and its number on the CD.

The CD also includes a recording grid on which you can indicate whether individual children have achieved specific learning objectives. You may decide not to use all the assessments with every pupil. In some cases, you might feel that you already have sufficient evidence that a child has achieved the specific objective and so leave it out. You may also decide to complete the assessments in a different order from the order in this book.

By filling in the the recording grid you will be able to build a clear picture of an individual's strengths and weaknesses as well as the class as a whole. The recording grid can be used to form an evidence base for assessing the National Curriculum level of each pupil, i.e. summative assessment. Your school or local authority will provide guidance regarding interpretation of evidence to make decisions about pupils' levels. Each pupil will be deemed to have reached a 'low', 'secure' or 'high' standard against the level criteria. Our recording grid uses these 'standards' (with red for 'low', orange for 'secure' and green for 'high') in relation to each 'I can' statement to help you make appropriate decisions about the progress of each pupil and how you might focus your teaching on each pupil's learning requirements.

Note that assessments are **not** provided for the following statements from the *Framework for mathematics* as these can be adequately covered in day-to-day experiences:

- Identify, visualise and describe properties of rectangles, triangles, regular polygons and 3-D solids

- Read, choose, use and record standard metric units to estimate and measure length, weight and capacity

- Read timetables and time using 24-hour clock notation

- Describe the occurrence of familiar events using the language of chance or likelihood

- Answer a set of related questions by collecting, selecting and organising relevant data

- Construct frequency tables, pictograms and bar and line graphs to represent the frequencies of events and changes over time; find and interpret the mode of a set of data

Count from any given number in whole-number and decimal steps (extending beyond zero when counting backwards; relate the numbers to their position on a number line)

Building on previous learning

Before starting this unit check that the children can already:

- recognise and continue number sequences formed by counting on or back in steps of constant size.

Learning objectives

Objective 1: Recognise and continue number sequences formed by counting on or back in whole-number or decimal steps of constant size.

Learning outcomes

The children will be able to:

- recognise and continue number sequences formed by counting *on* from any number in whole-number or decimal steps of constant size.
- recognise and continue number sequences formed by counting *back* from any number in whole-number or decimal steps of constant size.

Success criteria

The children have a **secure** level of attainment in relation to Objective 1 if the following question can be answered with a 'yes'.

Can the children...
... continue the sequences shown on the assessment sheet?

Administering the assessment

Ideally the children should work in a small group with an adult. Make sure that all the children understand the tasks. Ask individual pupils to explain what is happening in each sequence and to show the positions of the numbers on the class number line. Allow them ten minutes to complete the sheet, encouraging those who finish early to check that they have not made any mistakes. As an extension activity you could ask the children whether they think that the number 23.4 would fit in the sequence started in question 8 and to suggest a way that they could find this out.

(This assessment will also provide evidence for assessing strand 1, Using and applying mathematics: Explore patterns, properties and relationships and propose a general statement involving numbers or shapes; identify examples for which the statement is true or false; Explain reasoning using diagrams.)

Answers:		
1) 25, 27	2) 41, 43	3) 180, 183
4) 385, 381	5) 300, 250	6) 8.5, 9
7) 8, 7.5	8) 22.4, 22.5	9) 699, 696
10) 43.2, 43.5	11) 900, 902	12) 29.6, 29.5

Andrew Brodie: Ten Minute Maths Assessments ages 9–10 © A&C Black 2009

Count from any given number in whole-number and decimal steps

Name

Date

Look carefully at the number sequences. Write the next two numbers for each sequence. The first one has been done for you.

1. 17, 19, 21, 23, (25) , (27) , . . .

2. 33, 35, 37, 39, (   ) , (   ) , . . .

3. 168, 171, 174, 177, (   ) , (   ) , . . .

4. 401, 397, 393, 389, (   ) , (   ) , . . .

5. 500, 450, 400, 350, (   ) , (   ) , . . .

6. 6.5, 7, 7.5, 8, (   ) , (   ) , . . .

7. 10, 9.5, 9, 8.5, (   ) , (   ) , . . .

8. 22, 22.1, 22.2, 22.3, (   ) , (   ) , . . .

9. 711, 708, 705, 702, (   ) , (   ) , . . .

10. 42, 42.3, 42.6, 42.9, (   ) , (   ) , . . .

11. 892, 894, 896, 898, (   ) , (   ) , . . .

12. 30, 29.9, 29.8, 29.7, (   ) , (   ) , . . .

I can recognise and continue number sequences formed by counting **on** from any number in whole numbers or decimal steps of constant size.

I can recognise and continue number sequences formed by counting **back** from any number in whole numbers or decimal steps of constant size.

Partition whole numbers and decimals with up to two places

Building on previous learning

Before starting this unit check that the children can already:
- partition any four-digit number into multiples of 1000, 100, 10 and 1 in a variety of ways.

Learning objectives

Objective 1: Partition whole numbers and decimals with up to two places.

Learning outcomes

The children will be able to:
- explain what each digit represents in whole numbers and decimals with up to two places.
- partition whole numbers and decimals with up to two places into multiples of 10, 1, $\frac{1}{10}$ and $\frac{1}{100}$ in a variety of ways.

Success criteria

The children have a **secure** level of attainment in relation to Objective 1 if the following question can be answered with a 'yes'.

Can the children…
… partition the numbers shown on the assessment sheet in three different ways, confidently and quickly?

Administering the assessment

The ability to partition numbers helps pupils to understand other arithmetical processes, particularly the process of subtraction by decomposition. The children should be able to partition whole numbers and decimals with up to two places into multiples of 10, 1, $\frac{1}{10}$ and $\frac{1}{100}$ in a variety of ways e.g. a number such as 7.45 could be partitioned into: 7 + 0.4 + 0.05 or 6 + 1.4 + 0.05 or 7 + 0.3 + 0.15 or 6 + 1.3 + 0.15, etc. You could give the pupils this example before asking them to complete the assessment sheet. Encourage them to understand that there are lots of different ways of partitioning but that the total value of the number remains constant. Some pupils may have difficulty reading the questions on the sheet but nevertheless have the ability to complete the mathematics. Help these pupils with reading, encouraging them to discuss the mathematical processes.

Some schools use the term 'ones' rather than 'units' – ensure that the pupils understand that 'units' means 'ones'.

(This assessment will also provide evidence for assessing strand 1, Using and applying mathematics: Explore patterns, properties and relationships and propose a general statement involving numbers or shapes; identify examples for which the statement is true or false; Explain reasoning using diagrams.)

Answers: *There are various ways in which the pupils could split the numbers – check that all of the ways that they show are valid.*

Partition whole numbers and decimals with up to two places

Name

Date

Look at this number:

23.7

We can split it into tens, units and tenths in lots of ways.
Here are three examples of how the number could be split:

20 + 3 + 0.7   10 + 13 + 0.7   20 + 2 + 1.7

Split each of these numbers in three different ways.

34.8

42.9

3.62

9.25

53.84

65.34

I can find different ways to partition whole numbers and decimals with up to two places.

Round whole numbers and decimals with up to two places

Building on previous learning

Before starting this unit check that the children can already:

- read, write and order whole numbers to at least 1000 and position them on a number line.
- partition whole numbers and decimals with up to two places.

Learning objectives

Objective 1: Round whole numbers and decimals with up to two places to the nearest 10, 1 or $\frac{1}{10}$.

Learning outcomes

The children will be able to:

- explain what each digit represents in whole numbers and decimals with up to two places.
- round up or down whole numbers and decimals with up to two places to the nearest 10, 1 or $\frac{1}{10}$.

Success criteria

The children have a **secure** level of attainment in relation to Objective 1 if the following questions can be answered with a 'yes'.

Can the children…

… recognise that numbers such as 28.4, 6.9 and 2.48 can be rounded *up* to the nearest multiple of 10, 1 or $\frac{1}{10}$ respectively, to give an approximation?

… recognise that numbers such as 32.9, 12.3 and 3.61 can be rounded *down* to the nearest multiple of 10, 1 or $\frac{1}{10}$ respectively, to give an approximation?

… recognise that numbers such as 45, 7.5 and 4.65 can be rounded *up* to the nearest multiple of 10, 1 or $\frac{1}{10}$ respectively to give an approximation?

Administering the assessment

🔘 Track 1   Ideally the children should work in a small group with an adult. Ensure that they understand the tasks. Each child needs to be aware that, when rounding to the nearest 10, the *units* digit is more important than the *tenths* digit and that, when rounding to the nearest 1, the *tenths* digit is more important than the *hundredths* digit. S/he will also need to know that we always round up from multiples of 5 when rounding to the nearest 10, from multiples of 0.5 when rounding to the nearest 1 and from multiples of 0.05 when rounding to the nearest $\frac{1}{10}$. For the first part of the assessment the children have to write approximations of numbers shown on the sheet. For the second part you need the CD. This is the script for the CD if you decide to dictate the questions.

Find box a. Round 59 to the nearest 10 and write it in box a.
Round 62.3 to the nearest 10 and write it in box b.
Round 8.9 to the nearest whole number and write it in box c.
Round 11.2 to the nearest whole number and write it in box d.
Round 6.39 to the nearest tenth and write it in box e.
Round 7.52 to the nearest tenth and write it in box f.

(This assessment will also provide evidence for assessing strand 1, Using and applying mathematics: Explore patterns, properties and relationships and propose a general statement involving numbers or shapes; identify examples for which the statement is true or false; Explain reasoning using diagrams.)

Answers: 40 170 30 30 50
          7 12 128 80 8
          2.5 3.6 18.4 142.7 4.7
CD answers: 60, 60, 9, 11, 6.4, 7.5

Andrew Brodie: Ten Minute Maths Assessments ages 9–10 © A&C Black 2009

Round whole numbers and decimals with up to two places

Name

Date

Round these numbers to the nearest 10.

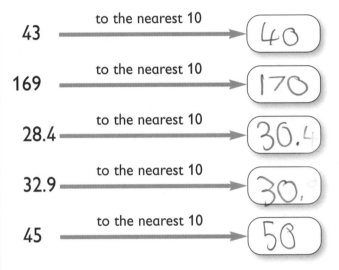

43 — to the nearest 10 → 40

169 — to the nearest 10 → 170

28.4 — to the nearest 10 → 30.4

32.9 — to the nearest 10 → 30,

45 — to the nearest 10 → 50

Round these numbers to the nearest tenth.

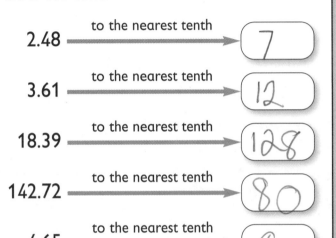

2.48 — to the nearest tenth → 7

3.61 — to the nearest tenth → 12

18.39 — to the nearest tenth → 128

142.72 — to the nearest tenth → 80

4.65 — to the nearest tenth → 8

Round these numbers to the nearest whole number.

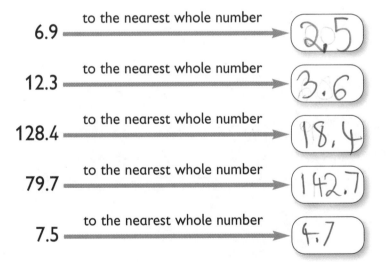

6.9 — to the nearest whole number → 2,5

12.3 — to the nearest whole number → 3.6

128.4 — to the nearest whole number → 18,4

79.7 — to the nearest whole number → 142.7

7.5 — to the nearest whole number → 4,7

Listen carefully and write the answers in the boxes.

a  60
b  60
c  9
d  11
e 6,4
f 7,5

I can round numbers to the nearest ten, whole number or tenth.

Order whole numbers and decimals with up to two places

Building on previous learning

Before starting this unit check that the children can already:

- read, write and order whole numbers to at least 1000 and position them on a number line.
- partition or round whole numbers and decimals with up to two places.

Learning objectives

Objective 1: Order whole numbers and decimals with up to two places.

Learning outcomes

The children will be able to:

- explain what each digit represents in whole numbers and decimals with up to two places.
- write sets of whole numbers and decimals with up to two places in order.
- create whole numbers and decimals with up to two places from separate digits by following given criteria.

Success criteria

The children have a **secure** level of attainment in relation to Objective 1 if the following questions can be answered with a 'yes'.

Can the children…

… write the sets of numbers shown on the assessment sheet in order?

… create the largest possible or smallest possible number incorporating two decimal places from the digits provided on the assessment sheet?

Administering the assessment

Ideally the children should work in a small group with an adult. You may decide to use the opportunity to assess pupils' knowledge and skills in rounding the numbers shown on the assessment sheet to the nearest 10, 1 or $\frac{1}{10}$. Encourage the pupils to discuss the assessment sheet, explaining the place values of the digits in the numbers. When you are confident that they are ready, allow them to complete the written tasks.

(This assessment will also provide evidence for assessing strand 1, Using and applying mathematics: Explore patterns, properties and relationships and propose a general statement involving numbers or shapes; identify examples for which the statement is true or false; Explain reasoning using diagrams; Represent a puzzle or problem by identifying and recording the information or calculations needed to solve it; find possible solutions and confirm them in the context of the problem.)

Answers:	3.6	3.65	3.7	6.35
	2.24	2.4	2.42	4.22
	7.3	7.39	9.37	9.73
	4.9	5	5.09	5.1
	96.42	24.69	964.2	246.9

Andrew Brodie: Ten Minute Maths Assessments ages 9–10 © A&C Black 2009

Order whole numbers and decimals with up to two places

Name

Date

Write each set of numbers in order, starting with the smallest.

| 3.65 | 6.35 | 3.7 | 3.6 |

------------------ ------------------ ------------------ ------------------

| 4.22 | 2.42 | 2.24 | 2.4 |

------------------ ------------------ ------------------ ------------------

| 9.73 | 9.37 | 7.39 | 7.3 |

------------------ ------------------ ------------------ ------------------

| 5 | 4.9 | 5.09 | 5.1 |

------------------ ------------------ ------------------ ------------------

Look at the four digit cards.

| **6** | **2** | **9** | **4** |

Using each digit only once, write the
largest possible number that has two decimal places.   ------------------

Using each digit only once, write the
smallest possible number that has two decimal places.   ------------------

Using each digit only once, write the
largest possible number that has one decimal place.   ------------------

Using each digit only once, write the
smallest possible number that has one decimal place.   ------------------

I can write numbers including decimals in order.

Express a smaller number as a fraction of a larger one

Building on previous learning

Before starting this unit check that the children can already:

- read and write proper fractions interpreting the denominator as the parts of a whole and the numerator as the number of parts.
- identify fractions shown on diagrams and match these to equivalent fractions on other diagrams.

Learning objectives

Objective 1: Express a smaller number as a fraction of a larger one e.g. recognise that 5 out of 8 is $\frac{5}{8}$.

Learning outcomes

The children will be able to:

- express a smaller number as a fraction of a larger one.
- use appropriate vocabulary related to fractions: numerator, denominator, half, quarter, eighth, third, sixth, ninth, twelfth, fifth, tenth, twentieth, hundredth, equivalent.

Success criteria

The children have a **secure** level of attainment in relation to Objective 1 if the following questions can be answered with a 'yes'.

Can the children...

... write the correct fraction for each question on the assessment sheet?

... label the fraction appropriately with the words denominator and numerator?

Administering the assessment

Ensure that the children understand how to complete the assessment sheet. Discuss each fraction with them. This assessment focuses on the task of expressing a smaller number as a fraction of a larger one but it also provides an opportunity to consider equivalent fractions e.g. in answering the first question the children would be correct with the answer $\frac{5}{20}$ but could be encouraged to realise that this is equivalent to $\frac{1}{4}$.

(This assessment will also provide evidence for assessing strand 1, Using and applying mathematics: Explore patterns, properties and relationships and propose a general statement involving numbers or shapes; identify examples for which the statement is true or false; Explain reasoning using diagrams and text; refine ways of recording using images and symbols; Represent a puzzle or problem by identifying and recording the information or calculations needed to solve it; find possible solutions and confirm them in the context of the problem.)

Answers: $\frac{5}{20}$ or $\frac{1}{4}$ $\frac{3}{20}$ $\frac{2}{20}$ or $\frac{1}{10}$ $\frac{10}{20}$ or $\frac{1}{2}$

$\frac{3}{9}$ or $\frac{1}{3}$ $\frac{6}{9}$ or $\frac{2}{3}$ $\frac{2}{9}$ $\frac{5}{9}$

$\frac{5}{12}$ $\begin{array}{l}\text{numerator}\\\text{denominator}\end{array}$

Express a smaller number as a fraction of a larger one

Name

Date

What fraction of the circles are black?

What fraction of the circles are grey?

What fraction of the circles have stripes?

What fraction of the circles have spots?

What fraction of the squares are black?

What fraction of the squares are grey?

What fraction of the squares would two squares be?

What fraction of the squares would five squares be?

Label the fraction below correctly using the words denominator and numerator.

$$\frac{5}{12}$$

I can express a smaller number as a fraction of a larger one.

Find equivalent fractions (1)

Building on previous learning

Before starting this unit check that the children can already:
- read and write proper fractions interpreting the denominator as the parts of a whole and the numerator as the number of parts.
- identify fractions shown on diagrams and match these to equivalent fractions on other diagrams.
- express a smaller number as a fraction of a larger one (e.g. recognise that 5 out of 8 is $\frac{5}{8}$).

Learning objectives

Objective 1: Find equivalent fractions (e.g. $\frac{7}{10} = \frac{14}{20}$).

Learning outcomes

The children will be able to:
- match fractions to their equivalents.
- use appropriate vocabulary related to fractions: numerator, denominator, half, quarter, eighth, third, sixth, ninth, twelfth, fifth, tenth, twentieth, hundredth, equivalent.

Success criteria

The children have a **secure** level of attainment in relation to Objective 1 if the following question can be answered with a 'yes'.

Can the children...
... match the fractions on the assessment sheet appropriately?

Administering the assessment

Ensure that the children understand how to complete the assessment sheet and that the second activity involves matching a fraction from each column. Discuss each fraction with them, ensuring that the children use the appropriate vocabulary.

(This assessment will also provide evidence for assessing strand 1, Using and applying mathematics: Explore patterns, properties and relationships and propose a general statement involving numbers or shapes; identify examples for which the statement is true or false; Explain reasoning using diagrams and text; refine ways of recording using images and symbols; Represent a puzzle or problem by identifying and recording the information or calculations needed to solve it; find possible solutions and confirm them in the context of the problem.)

Answers:

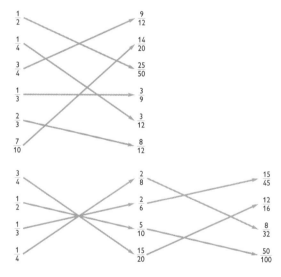

Andrew Brodie: Ten Minute Maths Assessments ages 9–10 © A&C Black 2009

Find equivalent fractions (1)

Name

Date

Draw lines to match each fraction on the left to its equivalent on the right.

$\dfrac{1}{2}$ $\dfrac{9}{12}$

$\dfrac{1}{4}$ $\dfrac{14}{20}$

$\dfrac{3}{4}$ $\dfrac{25}{50}$

$\dfrac{1}{3}$ $\dfrac{3}{9}$

$\dfrac{2}{3}$ $\dfrac{3}{12}$

$\dfrac{7}{10}$ $\dfrac{8}{12}$

$\dfrac{3}{4}$ $\dfrac{2}{8}$ $\dfrac{15}{45}$

$\dfrac{1}{2}$ $\dfrac{2}{6}$ $\dfrac{12}{16}$

$\dfrac{1}{3}$ $\dfrac{5}{10}$ $\dfrac{8}{32}$

$\dfrac{1}{4}$ $\dfrac{15}{20}$ $\dfrac{50}{100}$

I can find equivalent fractions.

Andrew Brodie: Ten Minute Maths Assessments ages 9–10 © A&C Black 2009

Find equivalent fractions (2)

Building on previous learning

Before starting this unit check that the children can already:

- read and write proper fractions interpreting the denominator as the *parts of a whole* and the numerator as the *number of parts*.
- identify fractions shown on diagrams and match these to equivalent fractions on other diagrams.
- express a smaller number as a fraction of a larger one (e.g. recognise that 5 out of 8 is $\frac{5}{8}$).
- find equivalent fractions (e.g. $\frac{7}{10} = \frac{14}{20}$).

Learning objectives

Objective 1: Find equivalent fractions, identifying the appropriate mixed number to match each improper fraction (e.g. $\frac{19}{10} = 1\frac{9}{10}$).

Learning outcomes

The children will be able to:

- match improper fractions to their equivalent mixed numbers.
- use appropriate vocabulary related to fractions: numerator, denominator, half, quarter, eighth, third, sixth, ninth, twelfth, fifth, tenth, twentieth, hundredth, equivalent, mixed number, proper fraction, improper fraction.

Success criteria

The children have a **secure** level of attainment in relation to Objective 1 if the following question can be answered with a 'yes'.

Can the children...
... match the fractions on the assessment sheet appropriately?

Administering the assessment

Ensure that the children understand how to complete the assessment sheet. Discuss each fraction with them, ensuring that the children use the appropriate vocabulary.

(This assessment will also provide evidence for assessing strand 1, Using and applying mathematics: Explore patterns, properties and relationships and propose a general statement involving numbers or shapes; identify examples for which the statement is true or false; Explain reasoning using diagrams and text; refine ways of recording using images and symbols; Represent a puzzle or problem by identifying and recording the information or calculations needed to solve it; find possible solutions and confirm them in the context of the problem.)

Answers:

$1\frac{1}{2}$ — $\frac{4}{3}$
$2\frac{3}{4}$ — $\frac{3}{2}$
$1\frac{1}{3}$ — $\frac{19}{10}$
$1\frac{9}{10}$ — $\frac{11}{4}$

$\frac{9}{8}$ — $1\frac{3}{7}$
$\frac{14}{4}$ — $1\frac{3}{4}$
$\frac{10}{7}$ — $1\frac{1}{8}$
$\frac{7}{4}$ — $3\frac{1}{2}$

Andrew Brodie: Ten Minute Maths Assessments ages 9–10 © A&C Black 2009

Find equivalent fractions (2)

Name

Date

Use the words **proper fraction**, **improper fraction** and **mixed number** to label each of these three fractions:

$\frac{11}{8}$ _____ $\frac{5}{8}$ _____ $1\frac{1}{8}$ _____

Draw lines to match the mixed numbers to the equivalent improper fractions.

$1\frac{1}{2}$ $\frac{4}{3}$

$2\frac{3}{4}$ $\frac{3}{2}$

$1\frac{1}{3}$ $\frac{19}{10}$

$1\frac{9}{10}$ $\frac{11}{4}$

Draw lines to match the mixed numbers to the equivalent improper fractions.

$\frac{9}{8}$ $1\frac{3}{7}$

$\frac{14}{4}$ $1\frac{3}{4}$

$\frac{10}{7}$ $1\frac{1}{8}$

$\frac{7}{4}$ $3\frac{1}{2}$

I can use the correct vocabulary for proper fractions, improper fractions and mixed numbers.

I can find improper fractions that are equivalent to mixed numbers.

I can find mixed numbers that are equivalent to improper fractions.

Relate fractions to their decimal representations

Building on previous learning

Before starting this unit check that the children can already:

- read and write proper fractions interpreting the denominator as the parts of a whole and the numerator as the number of parts.
- identify fractions shown on diagrams and match these to equivalent fractions on other diagrams.
- express a smaller number as a fraction of a larger one (e.g. recognise that 5 out of 8 is $\frac{5}{8}$).
- find equivalent fractions (e.g. $\frac{7}{10} = \frac{14}{20}$ or $\frac{19}{10} = 1\frac{9}{10}$).
- use decimal notation for tenths and hundredths.

Learning objectives

Objective 1: Relate fractions to their decimal representations.

Learning outcomes

The children will be able to:

- match fractions to their decimal representations.

Success criteria

The children have a **secure** level of attainment in relation to Objective 1 if the following question can be answered with a 'yes'.

Can the children...

... match the fractions to the decimal numbers on the assessment sheet appropriately?

Administering the assessment

Ensure that the children understand how to complete the assessment sheet. Discuss each fraction with them, ensuring that the children use the appropriate vocabulary. For the final task on the assessment sheet accept the answers shown below or appropriate equivalent fractions e.g. for 0.2 the children may write $\frac{2}{10}$ or they may write $\frac{1}{5}$.

(This assessment will also provide evidence for assessing strand 1, Using and applying mathematics: Explore patterns, properties and relationships and propose a general statement involving numbers or shapes; identify examples for which the statement is true or false; Explain reasoning using diagrams and text; refine ways of recording using images and symbols; Represent a puzzle or problem by identifying and recording the information or calculations needed to solve it; find possible solutions and confirm them in the context of the problem.)

Answers:

$\frac{9}{100} = 0.09$	$\frac{8}{10} = 0.8$	$\frac{72}{100} = 0.72$
$\frac{7}{10} = 0.7$	$\frac{55}{100} = 0.55$	$\frac{39}{100} = 0.39$
$\frac{3}{4} = 0.75$	$\frac{4}{10} = 0.4$	$\frac{34}{100} = 0.34$
$\frac{1}{2} = 0.5$	$\frac{95}{100} = 0.95$	$\frac{1}{4} = 0.25$
$\frac{6}{100} = 0.06$	$\frac{42}{100} = 0.42$	
$0.2 = \frac{2}{10}$	$0.4 = \frac{4}{10}$	$0.1 = \frac{1}{10}$
$0.51 = \frac{51}{100}$	$0.99 = \frac{99}{100}$	$0.83 = \frac{83}{100}$
$0.75 = \frac{3}{4}$		

Relate fractions to their decimal representations

Name

Date

Write the correct decimal number for each fraction.
Here are the decimal numbers you will need:

0.7   0.39   0.8   0.55   0.09   0.72

$\frac{9}{100}$ = ☐ $\frac{8}{10}$ = ☐ $\frac{72}{100}$ = ☐

$\frac{7}{10}$ = ☐ $\frac{55}{100}$ = ☐ $\frac{39}{100}$ = ☐

Write the correct decimal number for each fraction.
Here are the decimal numbers you will need:

0.4   0.42   0.5   0.95   0.06   0.25   0.75   0.34

$\frac{3}{4}$ = ☐ $\frac{4}{10}$ = ☐ $\frac{34}{100}$ = ☐

$\frac{1}{2}$ = ☐ $\frac{95}{100}$ = ☐ $\frac{1}{4}$ = ☐

$\frac{6}{100}$ = ☐ $\frac{42}{100}$ = ☐

Write the correct fraction for each decimal number.

0.2 = ☐   0.4 = ☐   0.1 = ☐   0.51 = ☐

0.51 = ☐   0.99 = ☐   0.83 = ☐   0.75 = ☐

I can match fractions to their decimal equivalents. ☐

Andrew Brodie: Ten Minute Maths Assessments ages 9–10 © A&C Black 2009

Understand percentage as the number of parts in every 100 and express tenths and hundredths as percentages

Building on previous learning

Before starting this unit check that the children can already:

- read and write proper fractions interpreting the denominator as the parts of a whole and the numerator as the number of parts.
- use decimal notation for tenths and hundredths.

Learning objectives

Objective 1: Understand percentage as the number of parts in every 100.
Objective 2: Express tenths and hundredths as percentages.

Learning outcomes

The children will be able to:

- express numbers of parts in every 100 as percentages.
- express half, quarter and three-quarters as percentages.
- express tenths and hundredths as percentages.

Success criteria

The children have a **secure** level of attainment in relation to Objective 1 if the following questions can be answered with a 'yes'.

Can the children…

… recognise the necessity to count the zebras and lions shown on the assessment sheet in order to represent each group as a percentage of the whole set?
… realise that the number of giraffes and elephants can be expressed as 50% and 25% respectively?
… write the fractions shown as percentages?

Administering the assessment

Discuss the illustration with the children. Are they able to explain percentages as the number of parts per 100? Do they understand that $\frac{1}{2}$ is 50% because $\frac{50}{100}$ is equivalent to $\frac{1}{2}$ and that $\frac{1}{4}$ is 25% because $\frac{25}{100}$ is equivalent to $\frac{1}{4}$?

(This assessment will also provide evidence for assessing strand 1, Using and applying mathematics: Explore patterns, properties and relationships and propose a general statement involving numbers or shapes; identify examples for which the statement is true or false; Explain reasoning using diagrams and text; refine ways of recording using images and symbols; Represent a puzzle or problem by identifying and recording the information or calculations needed to solve it; find possible solutions and confirm them in the context of the problem.)

Answers:	10%	15%	25%	50%	
	50%	25%	75%	10%	20%
	90%	17%	63%	5%	

Understand percentages

Here are 100 animals.
Half of them are giraffes and a quarter of them are elephants.

What percentage of the animals are zebras?

What percentage of the animals are elephants?

What percentage of the animals are lions?

What percentage of the animals are giraffes?

Write these fractions as percentages:

$\frac{1}{2}$ =

$\frac{1}{4}$ =

$\frac{3}{4}$ =

$\frac{1}{10}$ =

$\frac{2}{10}$ =

$\frac{9}{10}$ =

$\frac{17}{100}$ =

$\frac{63}{100}$ =

$\frac{5}{100}$ =

I can understand percentage as the number of parts in every 100.

I can express tenths and hundredths as percentages.

Solve problems involving proportions of quantities

Building on previous learning

Before starting this unit check that the children can already:

- read and write proper fractions interpreting the denominator as the parts of a whole and the numerator as the number of parts.
- find confidently half of 100.
- solve one-step and two-step problems involving numbers, money or measures.

Learning objectives

Objective 1: Solve problems involving proportions of quantities.

Learning outcomes

The children will be able to:

- solve one-step and two-step problems involving whole numbers and fractions.
- solve problems involving proportions of quantities.

Success criteria

The children have a **secure** level of attainment in relation to Objective 1 if the following questions can be answered with a 'yes'.

Can the children…

… quickly find the appropriate quantities of each ingredient to make half the quantity?

… realise that 18 is one and a half times 12 and use this knowledge to find the appropriate quantities?

Administering the assessment

Discuss the recipe with the children. As an extension activity you could make the cakes with them! Use the opportunity to remind the children of health and safety issues in relation to cooking.

(This assessment will also provide evidence for assessing strand 1, Using and applying mathematics: Solve one-step and two-step problems involving whole numbers and fractions, choosing and using appropriate calculation strategies; Explore patterns, properties and relationships and propose a general statement involving numbers or shapes; identify examples for which the statement is true or false; Explain reasoning using diagrams and text; refine ways of recording using images and symbols; Represent a puzzle or problem by identifying and recording the information or calculations needed to solve it; find possible solutions and confirm them in the context of the problem.)

Answers: 1 egg, 50 grams of self-raising flour, 50 grams of caster sugar, 50 grams of butter, $\frac{1}{2}$ level teaspoon of baking powder.
3 eggs, 150 grams of self-raising flour, 150 grams of caster sugar, 150 grams of butter, $1\frac{1}{2}$ level teaspoons of baking powder.

Solve problems involving proportions of quantities

Name

Date

Look at this recipe for making 12 small sponge cakes.

Simply super sponges

Ingredients:
2 eggs
100 grams of self-raising
    flour
100 grams of caster
    sugar
100 grams of butter
1 level teaspoon of
    baking powder

Method:
1. Pre-heat oven to 170°C.
2. Place paper cake cases in a patty-tin.
3. Put all your ingredients into a mixing bowl. Use an electric mixer to beat ingredients together for about 2 minutes.
4. Put a heaped teaspoonful of the mixture into each paper cake case.
5. Carefully place the patty-tin into the oven.
6. Leave for fifteen minutes or until golden brown.
7. Carefully remove from oven. Leave to cool.

Write the list of ingredients that you would need if you wanted to make just six of the cakes.

Write the list of ingredients that you would need if you wanted to make eighteen of the cakes.

I can solve problems involving proportions of quantities.

Use knowledge of place value and addition of two-digit numbers to derive sums of decimals

Building on previous learning

Before starting this unit check that the children can already:
- derive and recall all addition and subtraction facts for each number to 20.
- add mentally pairs of two-digit whole numbers.

Learning objectives

Objective 1: Derive sums of decimals.

Learning outcomes

The children will be able to:
- use their knowledge of addition facts and of place value to work out the sums of pairs of decimals.

Success criteria

The children have a **secure** level of attainment in relation to Objective 1 if the following question can be answered with a 'yes'.

Can the children…
… respond quickly and accurately to questions such as 'What is the total of 2.6 and 1.5?'?

Administering the assessment

🔘 Track 2 At this stage the pupils have had considerable experience in deriving and recalling addition and subtraction facts for whole numbers. Before completing this assessment ensure that the pupils have had practice in adding decimals to whole numbers and decimals to decimals. The assessment relies on the use of the CD for a timed test where the children are given ten seconds to answer each question. The purpose of the limited time is to ensure that the children have some thinking time to derive the facts. The last four questions are extension activities. Ensure that the children have looked at the assessment sheet before they start the test to make sure they understand their answers need to be written in the boxes provided. The practice question will help with this. This is the script for the CD if you decide to dictate the questions. (Answers are provided after each question.)

I will say each question twice then you will have ten seconds to answer it.

Practice question: What is the total of 3 and 1.2?	4.2
Question 1: Add 7 to 3.9.	10.9
Question 2: What is 14 plus 3.5?	17.5
Question 3: What is the sum of 12 and 12.25?	24.25
Question 4: Add together 1.4 and 1.3	2.7
Question 5: What is the total of 2.5 and 1.5?	4
Question 6: 3.8 plus 1.4	5.2
Question 7: 6.7 add 3.3	10
Question 8: What is 8.2 plus 1.9?	10.1
Question 9: Increase 4.7 by 0.9	5.6
Question 10: Add 1.9 to 5.7	7.6
Question 11: What is the sum of 9.8 and 3.5	13.3
Question 12: Add together 17.5 and 8.5	26
Question 13: What is the total of 2.6 and 1.5?	4.1
Question 14: 8.6 plus 1.6	10.2
Question 15: 9.7 plus 4.6	14.3
Question 16: What is the sum of 4.9 and 3.1?	8
Question 17: What is the total of 5, 4.1 and 3.2?	12.3
Question 18: Add together 3.2, 6 and 1.8	11
Question 19: What is the sum of 12, 13.4 and 5.3?	30.7
Question 20: Add 3.2, 4.7 and 6.9	14.8

(This assessment will also provide evidence for assessing strand 1, Using and applying mathematics: Explore patterns, properties and relationships and propose a general statement involving numbers or shapes; identify examples for which the statement is true or false; Solve one-step and two-step problems involving whole numbers and decimals.)

Use knowledge of place value and addition of two-digit numbers to derive sums of decimals

Name

Date

Practice question. 3 1.2

1. 7 3.9

2. 14 3.5

3. 12 12.25

4. 1.4 1.3

5. 2.5 1.5

6. 3.8 1.4

7. 6.7 3.3

8. 8.2 1.9

9. 4.7 0.9

10. 1.9 5.7

11. 9.8 3.5

12. 17.5 8.5

13. 2.6 1.5

14. 8.6 1.6

15. 9.7 4.6

16. 4.9 3.1

17. 5 4.1 3.2

18. 3.2 6 1.8

19. 12 13.4 5.3

20. 3.2 4.7 6.9

I can derive sums of numbers with decimals.

Use knowledge of place value and subtraction of two-digit numbers to derive differences between decimals

Building on previous learning

Before starting this unit check that the children can already:
- derive and recall all addition and subtraction facts for each number to 20.
- add and subtract mentally pairs of two-digit whole numbers.

Learning objectives

Objective 1: Derive differences between decimals.

Learning outcomes

The children will be able to:
- use their knowledge of subtraction facts and of place value to work out the differences between pairs of decimals.

Success criteria

The children have a **secure** level of attainment in relation to Objective 1 if the following question can be answered with a 'yes'.

Can the children…
… respond quickly and accurately to questions such as 'What is the difference between 9.2 and 7.8?'?

Administering the assessment

● Track 3   At this stage the pupils have had considerable experience in deriving and recalling addition and subtraction facts for whole numbers. Before completing this assessment ensure that the pupils have had practice in subtracting decimals from whole numbers and decimals from decimals. The assessment relies on the use of the CD for a timed test where the children are given ten seconds to answer each question. The purpose of the limited time is to ensure that the children have some thinking time to derive the facts. Ensure that the children have looked at the assessment sheet before they start the test to make sure they understand that their answers need to be written in the boxes provided. The practice question will help with this. This is the script for the CD if you decide to dictate the questions. (The answers are provided after each question.)

I will say each question twice then you will have ten seconds to answer it.
Practice question: What is the difference between 5 and 1.2? 3.8
Question 1: What is the difference between 4 and 2.5? 1.5
Question 2: What is 10 minus 2.5? 7.5
Question 3: What is 10 take away 1.9? 8.1
Question 4: 3 minus 0.6 2.4
Question 5: 8 subtract 5.3 2.7
Question 6: 9 take away 4.5 4.5
Question 7: What is 12 minus 9.9? 2.1
Question 8: What is 20 take away 12.5 7.5
Question 9: What is the difference between 2.5 and 1.3? 1.2
Question 10: Subtract 3.9 from 5 1.1
Question 11: 6 minus 5.4 0.6
Question 12: Subtract 3.2 from 4.9 1.7
Question 13: 8.4 minus 3.1 5.3
Question 14: 9.9 take away 3.6 6.3
Question 15: What is the difference between 4.8 and 2.1? 2.7
Question 16: What is the difference between 3.7 and 3.5? 0.2
Question 17: 4.1 take away 2.5 1.6
Question 18: 3.3 minus 1.8 1.5
Question 19: 8.4 subtract 3.7 4.7
Question 20: What is the difference between 9.2 and 7.8? 1.4

(This assessment will also provide evidence for assessing strand 1, Using and applying mathematics: Explore patterns, properties and relationships and propose a general statement involving numbers or shapes; identify examples for which the statement is true or false; Solve one-step and two-step problems involving whole numbers and decimals.)

Use knowledge of place value and subtraction of two-digit numbers to derive differences between decimals

Name

Date

Practice question. 5 1.2 ⬚

1. ⬚ 4 2.5

2. ⬚ 10 2.5

3. ⬚ 10 1.9

4. ⬚ 3 0.6

5. ⬚ 8 5.3

6. ⬚ 9 4.5

7. ⬚ 12 9.9

8. ⬚ 20 12.5

9. ⬚ 2.5 1.3

10. ⬚ 3.9 5

11. ⬚ 6 5.4

12. ⬚ 3.2 4.9

13. ⬚ 8.4 3.1

14. ⬚ 9.9 3.6

15. ⬚ 4.8 2.1

16. ⬚ 3.7 3.5

17. ⬚ 4.1 2.5

18. ⬚ 3.3 1.8

19. ⬚ 8.4 3.7

20. ⬚ 9.2 7.8

I can derive differences between decimals. ⬚

Use knowledge of place value and addition of two-digit numbers to derive doubles of decimals

Building on previous learning

Before starting this unit check that the children can already:
- derive and recall all addition and subtraction facts for each number to 20.
- add mentally pairs of two-digit whole numbers.
- identify the doubles of two-digit numbers; use these to caculate doubles of multiples of 10 and 100 and derive the corresponding halves.

Learning objectives

Objective 1: Derive doubles of decimals.

Learning outcomes

The children will be able to:
- use their knowledge of addition facts and of place value to work out the doubles of decimals.

Success criteria

The children have a **secure** level of attainment in relation to Objective 1 if the following question can be answered with a 'yes'.

Can the children…

… respond quickly and accurately to questions such as 'What number is double 1.2?' or 'What number is double 0.34?'

Administering the assessment

🔘 Track 4   At this stage the pupils have had considerable experience in deriving and recalling addition and subtraction facts for whole numbers. Before completing this assessment ensure that the pupils have had practice in adding decimals to whole numbers and decimals to decimals. The assessment relies on the use of the CD for a timed test where the children are given ten seconds to answer each question. The purpose of the limited time is to ensure that the children have some thinking time to derive the facts. Make sure that the children understand their answers need to be written in the boxes provided on the sheet. The practice question will help with this. This is the script for the CD if you decide to dictate the questions. (The answers are provided after each question.)

I will say each question twice then you will have ten seconds to answer it.

Practice question: What number is double 0.5?	1
Question 1: What number is double 1.5?	3
Question 2: What number is double 2.5?	5
Question 3: Double 0.4	0.8
Question 4: Double 0.3	0.6
Question 5: Double 0.6	1.2
Question 6: Double 0.8	1.6
Question 7: Double 1.3	2.6
Question 8: Double 1.7	3.4
Question 9: Double 1.9	3.8
Question 10: Double 1.2	2.4
Question 11: Double 2.4	4.8
Question 12: Double 3.2	6.4
Question 13: Double 2.6	5.2
Question 14: Double 2.9	5.8
Question 15: Double 0.21	0.42
Question 16: Double 0.25	0.5
Question 17: Double 0.34	0.68
Question 18: Double 0.75	1.5
Question 19: Double 0.83	1.66
Question 20: Double 0.99	1.98

(This assessment will also provide evidence for assessing strand 1, Using and applying mathematics: Explore patterns, properties and relationships and propose a general statement involving numbers or shapes; identify examples for which the statement is true or false; Solve one-step and two-step problems involving whole numbers and decimals.)

Use knowledge of place value and addition of two-digit numbers to derive doubles of decimals

Name

Date

Practice question. 0.5

1.   1.5

2.   2.5

3.   0.4

4.   0.3

5.   0.6

6.   0.8

7.   1.3

8.   1.7

9.   1.9

10.   1.2

11.   2.4

12.   3.2

13.   2.6

14.   2.9

15.   0.21

16.   0.25

17.   0.34

18.   0.75

19.   0.83

20.   0.99

I can derive doubles of decimals.

Use knowledge of place value and addition of two-digit numbers to derive halves of decimals

Building on previous learning

Before starting this unit check that the children can already:

- derive and recall all addition and subtraction facts for each number to 20.
- add and subtract mentally pairs of two-digit whole numbers.
- identify the doubles of two-digit numbers; use these to caculate doubles of multiples of 10 and 100 and derive the corresponding halves.
- use knowledge of place value and addition of two-digit numbers to derive doubles of decimals.

Learning objectives

Objective 1: Derive halves of decimals.

Learning outcomes

The children will be able to:

- use their knowledge of addition facts, of place value and of doubles to work out the halves of decimals.

Success criteria

The children have a **secure** level of attainment in relation to Objective 1 if the following question can be answered with a 'yes'.

Can the children…

… respond quickly and accurately to questions such as 'What number is half of 0.48?' or 'What number is half of 5.6?'

Administering the assessment

🔘 **Track 5** At this stage the pupils have had considerable experience in deriving and recalling addition and subtraction facts for whole numbers. Before completing this assessment make sure that the pupils have had practice in adding decimals to whole numbers and decimals to decimals and deriving the corresponding subtractions. The assessment relies on the use of the CD for a timed test where the children are given ten seconds to answer each question. The purpose of the limited time is to ensure that the children have some thinking time to derive the facts. Ensure that the children have looked at the assessment sheet before they start the test to help them understand that their answers need to be written in the boxes provided. The practice question will help with this. This is the script for the CD if you decide to dictate the questions. (The answers are provided after each question.)

I will say each question twice then you will have ten seconds to answer it.

Practice question: What number is half of 1?	*0.5*
Question 1: What number is half of 3?	*1.5*
Question 2: What number is half of 5?	*2.5*
Question 3: Half of 13	*6.5*
Question 4: Half of 4.2	*2.1*
Question 5: Half of 6.8	*3.4*
Question 6: Half of 8.6	*4.3*
Question 7: Half of 10.4	*5.2*
Question 8: Half of 12.6	*6.3*
Question 9: Half of 3.2	*1.6*
Question 10: Half of 5.4	*2.7*
Question 11: Half of 9.6	*4.8*
Question 12: Half of 7.8	*3.9*
Question 13: Half of 0.48	*0.24*
Question 14: Half of 0.9	*0.45*
Question 15: Half of 0.32	*0.16*
Question 16: Half of 0.66	*0.33*
Question 17: Half of 0.56	*0.28*
Question 18: Half of 2.32	*1.16*
Question 19: Half of 1.32	*0.66*
Question 20: Half of 1.76	*0.88*

(This assessment will also provide evidence for assessing strand 1, Using and applying mathematics: Explore patterns, properties and relationships and propose a general statement involving numbers or shapes; identify examples for which the statement is true or false; Solve one-step and two-step problems involving whole numbers and decimals.)

Use knowledge of place value and addition of two-digit numbers to derive halves of decimals

Name

Date

Practice question. 1 ◻

1. ◻	3	**11.** ◻	9.6
2. ◻	5	**12.** ◻	7.8
3. ◻	13	**13.** ◻	0.48
4. ◻	4.2	**14.** ◻	0.9
5. ◻	6.8	**15.** ◻	0.32
6. ◻	8.6	**16.** ◻	0.66
7. ◻	10.4	**17.** ◻	0.56
8. ◻	12.6	**18.** ◻	2.32
9. ◻	3.2	**19.** ◻	1.32
10. ◻	5.4	**20.** ◻	1.76

I can derive halves of decimals. ◻

Recall quickly multiplication and division facts for the 2 times table

Building on previous learning

Before starting this unit check that the children can already:

- derive and recall multiplication facts for the 2 times table.

Learning objectives

Objective 1: Recall quickly multiplication facts for the 2 times table.

Objective 2: Derive and recall division facts for the 2 times table.

Learning outcomes

The children will be able to:

- recall quickly all multiplication facts for the 2 times table and use these to derive quickly the corresponding division facts.

Success criteria

The children have a **secure** level of attainment in relation to Objective 1 if the following question can be answered with a 'yes'.

Can the children…

… respond quickly and accurately to the questions on the CD?

Administering the assessment

Track 6   Ensure that the children understand the task. They should be able to answer the questions without the need to pause the CD as this assessment is concerned with rapid recall. This is the script for the CD if you decide to dictate the questions. (The answers are provided after each question.)

I will say each of the first ten questions twice then you will have three seconds to answer it.

Question 1: 3 times 2	6
Question 2: 9 times 2	18
Question 3: 8 times 2	16
Question 4: 7 times 2	14
Question 5: 2 times 2	4
Question 6: 6 times 2	12
Question 7: 10 times 2	20
Question 8: 0 times 2	0
Question 9: 4 times 2	8
Question 10: 5 times 2	10

I will say each of the next ten questions twice then you will have five seconds to answer it.

Question 11: 20 divided by 2	10
Question 12: 14 divided by 2	7
Question 13: 6 divided by 2	3
Question 14: 10 divided by 2	5
Question 15: 8 divided by 2	4
Question 16: 18 divided by 2	9
Question 17: 12 divided by 2	6
Question 18: 4 divided by 2	2
Question 19: 16 divided by 2	8
Question 20: 2 divided by 2	1

Andrew Brodie: Ten Minute Maths Assessments ages 9–10 © A&C Black 2009

Recall quickly multiplication and division facts for the 2 times table

Name

Date

Listen carefully to the questions and write the answers in the correct boxes.

1.

2.

3.

4.

5.

6.

7.

8.

9.

10.

11.

12.

13.

14.

15.

16.

17.

18.

19.

20.

I can recall quickly the multiplication facts for the 2 times table.

I can recall quickly the division facts for the 2 times table.

Andrew Brodie: Ten Minute Maths Assessments ages 9–10 © A&C Black 2009

Recall quickly multiplication and division facts for the 3 times table

Building on previous learning

Before starting this unit check that the children can already:
- derive and recall multiplication facts for the 3 times table.

Learning objectives

Objective 1: Recall quickly multiplication facts for the 3 times table.
Objective 2: Derive and recall division facts for the 3 times table.

Learning outcomes

The children will be able to:
- recall quickly all multiplication facts for the 3 times table and use these to derive quickly the corresponding division facts.

Success criteria

The children have a **secure** level of attainment in relation to Objective 1 if the following question can be answered with a 'yes'.

Can the children...
... respond quickly and accurately to the questions on the CD?

Administering the assessment

Track 7 Ensure that the children understand the task. They should be able to answer the questions without the need to pause the CD as this assessment is concerned with rapid recall. This is the script for the CD if you decide to dictate the questions. (The answers are provided after each question.)

I will say each of the first ten questions twice then you will have three seconds to answer it.

Question 1: 8 times 3	24
Question 2: 2 times 3	6
Question 3: 10 times 3	30
Question 4: 7 times 3	21
Question 5: 4 times 3	12
Question 6: 9 times 3	27
Question 7: 5 times 3	15
Question 8: 3 times 3	9
Question 9: 0 times 3	0
Question 10: 6 times 3	18

I will say each of the next ten questions twice then you will have five seconds to answer it.

Question 11: 15 divided by 3	5
Question 12: 24 divided by 3	8
Question 13: 9 divided by 3	3
Question 14: 3 divided by 3	1
Question 15: 12 divided by 3	4
Question 16: 18 divided by 3	6
Question 17: 27 divided by 3	9
Question 18: 30 divided by 3	10
Question 19: 21 divided by 3	7
Question 20: 6 divided by 3	2

Andrew Brodie: Ten Minute Maths Assessments ages 9–10 © A&C Black 2009

Recall quickly multiplication and division facts for the 3 times table

Name

Date

Listen carefully to the questions and write the answers in the correct boxes.

1.

2.

3.

4.

5.

6.

7.

8.

9.

10.

11.

12.

13.

14.

15.

16.

17.

18.

19.

20.

I can recall quickly the multiplication facts for the 3 times table.

I can recall quickly the division facts for the 3 times table.

Andrew Brodie: Ten Minute Maths Assessments ages 9–10 © A&C Black 2009

Recall quickly multiplication and division facts for the 4 times table

Building on previous learning

Before starting this unit check that the children can already:
- derive and recall multiplication facts for the 4 times table.

Learning objectives

Objective 1: Recall quickly multiplication facts for the 4 times table.
Objective 2: Derive and recall division facts for the 4 times table.

Learning outcomes

The children will be able to:
- recall quickly all multiplication facts for the 4 times table and use these to derive quickly the corresponding division facts.

Success criteria

The children have a **secure** level of attainment in relation to Objective 1 if the following question can be answered with a 'yes'.

Can the children...
... respond quickly and accurately to the questions on the CD?

Administering the assessment

🔘 Track 8   Ensure that the children understand the task. They should be able to answer the questions without the need to pause the CD as this assessment is concerned with rapid recall. This is the script for the CD if you decide to dictate the questions. (The answers are provided after each question.)

I will say each of the first ten questions twice then you will have three seconds to answer it.

Question 1: 6 times 4	24
Question 2: 10 times 4	40
Question 3: 0 times 4	0
Question 4: 3 times 4	12
Question 5: 9 times 4	36
Question 6: 2 times 4	8
Question 7: 8 times 4	32
Question 8: 4 times 4	16
Question 9: 7 times 4	28
Question 10: 5 times 4	20

I will say each of the next ten questions twice then you will have five seconds to answer it.

Question 11: 20 divided by 4	5
Question 12: 32 divided by 4	8
Question 13: 16 divided by 4	4
Question 14: 8 divided by 4	2
Question 15: 28 divided by 4	7
Question 16: 36 divided by 4	9
Question 17: 4 divided by 4	1
Question 18: 40 divided by 4	10
Question 19: 12 divided by 4	3
Question 20: 24 divided by 4	6

Andrew Brodie: Ten Minute Maths Assessments ages 9–10 © A&C Black 2009

Recall quickly multiplication and division facts for the 4 times table

Name

Date

Listen carefully to the questions and write the answers in the correct boxes.

1.

2.

3.

4.

5.

6.

7.

8.

9.

10.

11.

12.

13.

14.

15.

16.

17.

18.

19.

20.

I can recall quickly the multiplication facts for the 4 times table.

I can recall quickly the division facts for the 4 times table.

Recall quickly multiplication and division facts for the 5 times table

Building on previous learning

Before starting this unit check that the children can already:

● derive and recall multiplication facts for the 5 times table.

Learning objectives

Objective 1: Recall quickly multiplication facts for the 5 times table.

Objective 2: Derive and recall division facts for the 5 times table.

Learning outcomes

The children will be able to:

● recall quickly all multiplication facts for the 5 times table and use these to derive quickly the corresponding division facts.

Success criteria

The children have a **secure** level of attainment in relation to Objective 1 if the following question can be answered with a 'yes'.

Can the children...

... respond quickly and accurately to the questions on the CD?

Administering the assessment

Track 9 Ensure that the children understand the task. They should be able to answer the questions without the need to pause the CD as this assessment is concerned with rapid recall. This is the script for the CD if you decide to dictate the questions. (The answers are provided after each question.)

I will say each of the first ten questions twice then you will have three seconds to answer it.

Question 1: 0 times 5	0
Question 2: 5 times 5	25
Question 3: 9 times 5	45
Question 4: 4 times 5	20
Question 5: 10 times 5	50
Question 6: 3 times 5	15
Question 7: 7 times 5	35
Question 8: 2 times 5	10
Question 9: 6 times 5	30
Question 10: 8 times 5	40

I will say each of the next ten questions twice then you will have five seconds to answer it.

Question 11: 20 divided by 5	4
Question 12: 50 divided by 5	10
Question 13: 35 divided by 5	7
Question 14: 5 divided by 5	1
Question 15: 25 divided by 5	5
Question 16: 10 divided by 5	2
Question 17: 45 divided by 5	9
Question 18: 30 divided by 5	6
Question 19: 15 divided by 5	3
Question 20: 40 divided by 5	8

Andrew Brodie: Ten Minute Maths Assessments ages 9–10 © A&C Black 2009

Recall quickly multiplication and division facts for the 5 times table

Name

Date

Listen carefully to the questions and write the answers in the correct boxes.

1. ☐

2. ☐

3. ☐

4. ☐

5. ☐

6. ☐

7. ☐

8. ☐

9. ☐

10. ☐

11. ☐

12. ☐

13. ☐

14. ☐

15. ☐

16. ☐

17. ☐

18. ☐

19. ☐

20. ☐

I can recall quickly the multiplication facts for the 5 times table. ☐

I can recall quickly the division facts for the 5 times table. ☐

Andrew Brodie: Ten Minute Maths Assessments ages 9–10 © A&C Black 2009

Recall quickly multiplication and division facts for the 6 times table

Building on previous learning

Before starting this unit check that the children can already:
- derive and recall multiplication facts for the 6 times table.

Learning objectives

Objective 1: Recall quickly multiplication facts for the 6 times table.
Objective 2: Derive and recall division facts for the 6 times table.

Learning outcomes

The children will be able to:
- recall quickly all multiplication facts for the 6 times table and use these to derive quickly the corresponding division facts.

Success criteria

The children have a **secure** level of attainment in relation to Objective 1 if the following question can be answered with a 'yes'.

Can the children...
... respond quickly and accurately to the questions on the CD?

Administering the assessment

Track 10 Ensure that the children understand the task. They should be able to answer the questions without the need to pause the CD as this assessment is concerned with rapid recall. This is the script for the CD if you decide to dictate the questions. (The answers are provided after each question.)

I will say each of the first ten questions twice then you will have three seconds to answer it.

Question 1:	8 times 6	48
Question 2:	0 times 6	0
Question 3:	2 times 6	12
Question 4:	9 times 6	54
Question 5:	3 times 6	18
Question 6:	5 times 6	30
Question 7:	6 times 6	36
Question 8:	10 times 6	60
Question 9:	7 times 6	42
Question 10:	4 times 6	24

I will say each of the next ten questions twice then you will have five seconds to answer it.

Question 11:	6 divided by 6	1
Question 12:	54 divided by 6	9
Question 13:	12 divided by 6	2
Question 14:	42 divided by 6	7
Question 15:	18 divided by 6	3
Question 16:	60 divided by 6	10
Question 17:	48 divided by 6	8
Question 18:	30 divided by 6	5
Question 19:	36 divided by 6	6
Question 20:	24 divided by 6	4

Andrew Brodie: Ten Minute Maths Assessments ages 9–10 © A&C Black 2009

Recall quickly multiplication and division facts for the 6 times table

Name

Date

Listen carefully to the questions and write the answers in the correct boxes.

1. ⬚

2. ⬚

3. ⬚

4. ⬚

5. ⬚

6. ⬚

7. ⬚

8. ⬚

9. ⬚

10. ⬚

11. ⬚

12. ⬚

13. ⬚

14. ⬚

15. ⬚

16. ⬚

17. ⬚

18. ⬚

19. ⬚

20. ⬚

I can recall quickly the multiplication facts for the 6 times table. ⬚

I can recall quickly the division facts for the 6 times table. ⬚

Recall quickly multiplication and division facts for the 7 times table

Building on previous learning

Before starting this unit check that the children can already:
- derive and recall multiplication facts for the 7 times table.

Learning objectives

Objective 1: Recall quickly multiplication facts for the 7 times table.
Objective 2: Derive and recall division facts for the 7 times table.

Learning outcomes

The children will be able to:
- recall quickly all multiplication facts for the 7 times table and use these to derive quickly the corresponding division facts.

Success criteria

The children have a **secure** level of attainment in relation to Objective 1 if the following question can be answered with a 'yes'.

Can the children...
... respond quickly and accurately to the questions on the CD?

Administering the assessment

● Track 11 Ensure that the children understand the task. They should be able to answer the questions without the need to pause the CD as this assessment is concerned with rapid recall. This is the script for the CD if you decide to dictate the questions. (The answers are provided after each question.)

I will say each of the first ten questions twice then you will have three seconds to answer it.

Question 1: 10 times 7	70
Question 2: 7 times 7	49
Question 3: 0 times 7	0
Question 4: 2 times 7	14
Question 5: 6 times 7	42
Question 6: 9 times 7	63
Question 7: 5 times 7	35
Question 8: 3 times 7	21
Question 9: 8 times 7	56
Question 10: 4 times 7	28

I will say each of the next ten questions twice then you will have five seconds to answer it.

Question 11: 56 divided by 7	8
Question 12: 70 divided by 7	10
Question 13: 7 divided by 7	1
Question 14: 21 divided by 7	3
Question 15: 35 divided by 7	5
Question 16: 63 divided by 7	9
Question 17: 28 divided by 7	4
Question 18: 14 divided by 7	2
Question 19: 42 divided by 7	6
Question 20: 49 divided by 7	7

Andrew Brodie: Ten Minute Maths Assessments ages 9–10 © A&C Black 2009

Recall quickly multiplication and division facts for the 7 times table

Name

Date

Listen carefully to the questions and write the answers in the correct boxes.

1. [ ]   11. [ ]

2. [ ]   12. [ ]

3. [ ]   13. [ ]

4. [ ]   14. [ ]

5. [ ]   15. [ ]

6. [ ]   16. [ ]

7. [ ]   17. [ ]

8. [ ]   18. [ ]

9. [ ]   19. [ ]

10. [ ]   20. [ ]

I can recall quickly the multiplication facts for the 7 times table. [ ]

I can recall quickly the division facts for the 7 times table. [ ]

Recall quickly multiplication and division facts for the 8 times table

Building on previous learning

Before starting this unit check that the children can already:
- derive and recall multiplication facts for the 8 times table.

Learning objectives

Objective 1: Recall quickly multiplication facts for the 8 times table.
Objective 2: Derive and recall division facts for the 8 times table.

Learning outcomes

The children will be able to:
- recall quickly all multiplication facts for the 8 times table and use these to derive quickly the corresponding division facts.

Success criteria

The children have a **secure** level of attainment in relation to Objective 1 if the following question can be answered with a 'yes'.

Can the children…
… respond quickly and accurately to the questions on the CD?

Administering the assessment

🔘 Track 12   Ensure that the children understand the task. They should be able to answer the questions without the need to pause the audio as this assessment is concerned with rapid recall. This is the script for the CD if you decide to dictate the questions. (The answers are provided after each question.)

I will say each of the first ten questions twice then you will have three seconds to answer it.

Question 1: 2 times 8	16
Question 2: 9 times 8	72
Question 3: 4 times 8	32
Question 4: 7 times 8	56
Question 5: 3 times 8	24
Question 6: 0 times 8	0
Question 7: 8 times 8	64
Question 8: 5 times 8	40
Question 9: 10 times 8	80
Question 10: 6 times 8	48

I will say each of the next ten questions twice then you will have five seconds to answer it.

Question 11: 64 divided by 8	8
Question 12: 80 divided by 8	10
Question 13: 8 divided by 8	1
Question 14: 32 divided by 8	4
Question 15: 48 divided by 8	6
Question 16: 72 divided by 8	9
Question 17: 16 divided by 8	2
Question 18: 40 divided by 8	5
Question 19: 24 divided by 8	3
Question 20: 56 divided by 8	7

Andrew Brodie: Ten Minute Maths Assessments ages 9–10 © A&C Black 2009

Recall quickly multiplication and division facts for the 8 times table

Name

Date

Listen carefully to the questions and write the answers in the correct boxes.

1.

2.

3.

4.

5.

6.

7.

8.

9.

10.

11.

12.

13.

14.

15.

16.

17.

18.

19.

20.

I can recall quickly the multiplication facts for the 8 times table.

I can recall quickly the division facts for the 8 times table.

Recall quickly multiplication and division facts for the 9 times table

Building on previous learning

Before starting this unit check that the children can already:
- derive and recall multiplication facts for the 9 times table.

Learning objectives

Objective 1: Recall quickly multiplication facts for the 9 times table.
Objective 2: Derive and recall division facts for the 9 times table.

Learning outcomes

The children will be able to:
- recall quickly all multiplication facts for the 9 times table and use these to derive quickly the corresponding division facts.

Success criteria

The children have a **secure** level of attainment in relation to Objective 1 if the following question can be answered with a 'yes'.

Can the children...
... respond quickly and accurately to the questions on the CD?

Administering the assessment

● Track 13 Ensure that the children understand the task. They should be able to answer the questions without the need to pause the audio as this assessment is concerned with rapid recall. This is the script for the CD if you decide to dictate the questions. (The answers are provided after each question.)

I will say each of the first ten questions twice then you will have three seconds to answer it.

Question 1: 6 times 9	54
Question 2: 9 times 9	81
Question 3: 0 times 9	0
Question 4: 5 times 9	45
Question 5: 7 times 9	63
Question 6: 4 times 9	36
Question 7: 8 times 9	72
Question 8: 5 times 9	45
Question 9: 10 times 9	90
Question 10: 2 times 9	18

I will say each of the next ten questions twice then you will have five seconds to answer it.

Question 11: 63 divided by 9	7
Question 12: 90 divided by 9	10
Question 13: 9 divided by 9	1
Question 14: 45 divided by 9	5
Question 15: 18 divided by 9	2
Question 16: 54 divided by 9	6
Question 17: 36 divided by 9	4
Question 18: 72 divided by 9	8
Question 19: 27 divided by 9	3
Question 20: 81 divided by 9	9

Andrew Brodie: Ten Minute Maths Assessments ages 9–10 © A&C Black 2009

Recall quickly multiplication and division facts for the 9 times table

Name

Date

Listen carefully to the questions and write the answers in the correct boxes.

1.

2.

3.

4.

5.

6.

7.

8.

9.

10.

11.

12.

13.

14.

15.

16.

17.

18.

19.

20.

I can recall quickly the multiplication facts for the 9 times table.

I can recall quickly the division facts for the 9 times table.

Recall quickly multiplication facts up to 10 x 10 and use them to multiply pairs of multiples of 10 and 100

Building on previous learning

Before starting this unit check that the children can already:
- recall quickly multiplication facts up to 10 x 10.

Learning objectives

Objective 1: Use multiplication facts up to 10 x 10 to multiply pairs of multiples of 10 and 100.

Learning outcomes

The children will be able to:
- recall quickly all multiplication facts up to 10 x 10 in order to multiply pairs of multiples of 10 and 100.

Success criteria

The children have a **secure** level of attainment in relation to Objective 1 if the following question can be answered with a 'yes'.

Can the children...
... respond quickly and accurately to the questions on the CD?

Administering the assessment

🔘 **Track 14** Ensure that the children understand the task. They should be able to answer the questions without the need to pause the audio as this assessment is concerned with rapid recall. This is the script for the CD if you decide to dictate the questions. (The answers are provided after each question.)

I will say each of the questions twice then you will have five seconds to answer it.

Question 1: 10 times 20	200
Question 2: 20 times 30	600
Question 3: 20 times 40	800
Question 4: 50 times 50	2500
Question 5: 60 times 30	1800
Question 6: 40 times 50	2000
Question 7: 70 times 30	2100
Question 8: 50 times 80	4000
Question 9: 20 times 90	1800
Question 10: 30 times 80	2400
Question 11: 20 times 100	2000
Question 12: 30 times 200	6000
Question 13: 50 times 500	25000
Question 14: 300 times 60	18000
Question 15: 400 times 70	28000
Question 16: 300 times 300	90000
Question 17: 400 times 600	240000
Question 18: 200 times 700	140000
Question 19: 800 times 900	720000
Question 20: 600 times 500	300000

Andrew Brodie: Ten Minute Maths Assessments ages 9–10 © A&C Black 2009

Recall quickly multiplication facts up to 10 x 10 and use them to multiply pairs of multiples of 10 and 100

Name

Date

Listen carefully to the questions and write the answers in the correct boxes.

1.

2.

3.

4.

5.

6.

7.

8.

9.

10.

11.

12.

13.

14.

15.

16.

17.

18.

19.

20.

I can multiply pairs of multiples of 10 and 100.

Recall quickly multiplication facts up to 10 x 10 and use them to divide pairs of multiples of 10 and 100

Building on previous learning

Before starting this unit check that the children can already:
- recall quickly multiplication facts up to 10 x 10 and derive the corresponding division facts.

Learning objectives

Objective 1: Use multiplication facts up to 10 x 10 to divide pairs of multiples of 10 and 100.

Learning outcomes

The children will be able to:
- recall quickly all multiplication facts up to 10 x 10 in order to divide pairs of multiples of 10 and 100.

Success criteria

The children have a **secure** level of attainment in relation to Objective 1 if the following question can be answered with a 'yes'.

Can the children...
... respond quickly and accurately to the questions on the CD?

Administering the assessment

🔘 Track 15 Ensure that the children understand the task. They should be able to answer the questions without the need to pause the CD as this assessment is concerned with rapid recall. This is the script for the CD if you decide to dictate the questions. (The answers are provided after each question.)

I will say each of the questions twice then you will have five seconds to answer it.

Question 1: 4000 divided by 80	50
Question 2: 900 divided by 30	30
Question 3: 600 divided by 30	20
Question 4: 1000 divided by 50	20
Question 5: 1200 divided by 20	60
Question 6: 2000 divided by 50	40
Question 7: 800 divided by 40	20
Question 8: 1400 divided by 20	70
Question 9: 1800 divided by 30	60
Question 10: 2100 divided by 70	30
Question 11: 8000 divided by 40	200
Question 12: 8100 divided by 90	90
Question 13: 12,000 divided by 40	300
Question 14: 16,000 divided by 20	800
Question 15: 24,000 divided by 30	800
Question 16: 20,000 divided by 50	400
Question 17: 36,000 divided by 400	90
Question 18: 100,000 divided by 200	500
Question 19: 210,000 divided by 300	700
Question 20: 150,000 divided by 500	300

Andrew Brodie: Ten Minute Maths Assessments ages 9–10 © A&C Black 2009

Recall quickly multiplication facts up to 10 x 10 and use them to divide pairs of multiples of 10 and 100

Name

Date

Listen carefully to the questions and write the answers in the correct boxes.

1.		4000	11.		8000
2.		900	12.		8100
3.		600	13.		12,000
4.		1000	14.		16,000
5.		1200	15.		24,000
6.		2000	16.		20,000
7.		800	17.		36,000
8.		1400	18.		100,000
9.		1800	19.		210,000
10.		2100	20.		150,000

I can divide pairs of multiples of 10 and 100.

Andrew Brodie: Ten Minute Maths Assessments ages 9–10 © A&C Black 2009

Identify pairs of factors of two-digit whole numbers

Building on previous learning

Before starting this unit check that the children can already:
- recall quickly multiplication facts up to 10 x 10 and derive the corresponding division facts.

Learning objectives

Objective 1: Identify pairs of factors of two-digit whole numbers.

Learning outcomes

The children will be able to:
- identify pairs of factors of two-digit whole numbers.
- state the factors for each two-digit number.
- recognise that prime numbers only have two factors, themselves and 1.

Success criteria

The children have a **secure** level of attainment in relation to Objective 1 if the following question can be answered with a 'yes'.

Can the children...
- ... find all the pairs of factors to complete the tasks on the worksheet, quickly and correctly?

Administering the assessment

Discuss the example with the children, ensuring that they understand why each number is there. Encourage them to discuss the factors of 8, then the factors of 16, noticing that as 16 is a square number, one line will have two identical numbers as the pair of factors.

As an extension activity you could discuss prime numbers, using the number 11 on the assessment sheet as an example.

(This assessment will also provide evidence for assessing strand 1, Using and applying mathematics: Solve one-step and two-step problems involving whole numbers and fractions, choosing and using appropriate calculation strategies; Explore patterns, properties and relationships and propose a general statement involving numbers or shapes; identify examples for which the statement is true or false; Explain reasoning using diagrams and text; refine ways of recording using images and symbols; Represent a puzzle or problem by identifying and recording the information or calculations needed to solve it; find possible solutions and confirm them in the context of the problem.)

Answers:	8:	16:	20:
	1 x 8	1 x 16	1 x 20
	8 x 1	16 x 1	20 x 1
	2 x 4	2 x 8	2 x 10
	4 x 2	8 x 2	10 x 2
		4 x 4	4 x 5
			5 x 4

	24:	40:	11:
	1 x 24	1 x 40	1 x 11
	24 x 1	40 x 1	11 x 1
	2 x 12	2 x 20	
	12 x 2	20 x 2	
	3 x 8	4 x 10	
	8 x 3	10 x 4	
	4 x 6	5 x 8	
	6 x 4	8 x 5	

Identify pairs of factors of two-digit whole numbers

Name

Date

Write the pairs of factors for each number below.
The first one has been done for you.

12	8	16	20
1 x 12			
12 x 1			
2 x 6			
6 x 2			
3 x 4			
4 x 3			

24	40	11

I can identify pairs of factors of two-digit whole numbers.

Find common multiples

Building on previous learning

Before starting this unit check that the children can already:

- recall quickly multiplication facts up to 10 x 10 and derive the corresponding division facts.

Learning objectives

Objective 1: Find common multiples (e.g. for 6 and 9).

Learning outcomes

The children will be able to:

- identify common multiples of pairs of one-digit numbers.

Success criteria

The children have a **secure** level of attainment in relation to Objective 1 if the following question can be answered with a 'yes'.

Can the children...

... rapidly identify the multiples up to 10 x of given one-digit numbers then compare the lists to find common multiples?

... record the results appropriately in a Venn diagram?

Administering the assessment

Discuss the first task with the pupils, ensuring that they remember the term 'multiples'. They may need to be reminded about Venn diagrams and shown how the overlapping area should contain the common multiples. You could extend the activity by asking for common multiples of other combinations of one-digit numbers e.g. 3 and 4, 4 and 6, 6 and 8, etc. Please note that multiples of 6 and 9 extend beyond the range of the multiplication tables. The answers shown below include those that appear in the tables as far as 10 x 9 and 10 x 5 respectively.

(This assessment will also provide evidence for assessing strand 1, Using and applying mathematics: Solve one-step and two-step problems involving whole numbers and fractions, choosing and using appropriate calculation strategies; Explore patterns, properties and relationships and propose a general statement involving numbers or shapes; identify examples for which the statement is true or false; Explain reasoning using diagrams and text; refine ways of recording using images and symbols; Represent a puzzle or problem by identifying and recording the information or calculations needed to solve it; find possible solutions and confirm them in the context of the problem.)

Answers: *6 12 18 24 30 36 42 48 54 60*
9 18 27 36 45 54 63 72 81 90

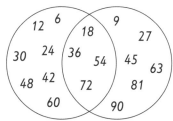

18 36 54 72

3 6 9 12 15 18 21 24 27 30
5 10 15 20 25 30 35 40 45 50

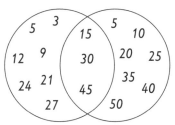

15 30 45

Find common multiples

Name

Date

Write the multiples of 6 up to 10 x 6.

------- ------- ------- ------- ------- ------- ------- ------- ------- -------

Write the multiples of 9 up to 10 x 9.

------- ------- ------- ------- ------- ------- ------- ------- ------- -------

Show your results on the Venn diagram.

multiples of 6   multiples of 9

Which numbers are common multiples of 6 and 9? ------- ------- ------- -------

Write the multiples of 3 up to 10 x 3.

------- ------- ------- ------- ------- ------- ------- ------- ------- -------

Write the multiples of 5 up to 10 x 5.

------- ------- ------- ------- ------- ------- ------- ------- ------- -------

Show your results on the Venn diagram.

multiples of 3   multiples of 5

Which numbers are common multiples of 3 and 5? ------- ------- -------

I can identify common multiples of one-digit numbers.

Extend mental methods for whole-number calculations (addition)

Building on previous learning

Before starting this unit check that the children can already:

- derive and recall all addition facts for each number to 20.
- derive and recall sums and differences of multiples of 10.
- derive and recall number pairs that total 100.
- identify the doubles of two-digit numbers.
- add mentally pairs of two-digit whole numbers.

Learning objectives

Objective 1: Use mental methods for adding whole numbers.

Learning outcomes

The children will be able to:

- use mental methods for an increasing range of additions.

Success criteria

The children have a **secure** level of attainment in relation to Objective 1 if the following question can be answered with a 'yes'.

Can the children…
… respond quickly and accurately to the questions?

Administering the assessment

Ensure that the children understand the task. Watch them carefully to see whether they have appropriate strategies for the calculations. Simple jottings should be allowed but this assessment is focused on mental methods and children should not use formal written methods. You can simply let the children work through the sheet at their own pace but you may prefer to dictate the questions below and limit the time allowed for each question to ten seconds.
(The answers are provided after each question.)

Question 1: 25 add 17	*42*
Question 2: 67 add 24	*91*
Question 3: 48 add 35	*83*
Question 4: 77 add 26	*103*
Question 5: 163 add 14	*177*
Question 6: 365 add 25	*390*
Question 7: 485 add 65	*550*
Question 8: 619 add 102	*721*
Question 9: 38 add 253	*291*
Question 10: 69 add 848	*917*
Question 11: 37 add 532	*569*
Question 12: 49 add 351	*400*
Question 13: 148 add 144	*292*
Question 14: 365 add 124	*489*
Question 15: 568 add 132	*700*
Question 16: 647 add 123	*770*
Question 17: 739 add 180	*919*
Question 18: 88 add 888	*976*
Question 19: 864 add 217	*1081*
Question 20: 948 add 357	*1305*

(This assessment will also provide evidence for assessing strand 1, Using and applying mathematics: Solve one-step and two-step problems involving whole numbers and fractions, choosing and using appropriate calculation strategies.)

Andrew Brodie: Ten Minute Maths Assessments ages 9–10 © A&C Black 2009

Extend mental methods for whole-number calculations (addition)

Name

Date

Write the answers in the correct boxes.

1. 25 + 17 =

11. 37 + 532 =

2. 67 + 24 =

12. 49 + 351 =

3. 48 + 35 =

13. 148 + 144 =

4. 77 + 26 =

14. 365 + 124 =

5. 163 + 14 =

15. 568 + 132 =

6. 365 + 25 =

16. 647 + 123 =

7. 485 + 65 =

17. 739 + 180 =

8. 619 + 102 =

18. 88 + 888 =

9. 38 + 253 =

19. 864 + 217 =

10. 69 + 848 =

20. 948 + 357 =

I can add numbers together mentally.

Extend mental methods for whole-number calculations (subtraction)

Building on previous learning

Before starting this unit check that the children can already:
- derive and recall all addition and subtraction facts for each number to 20.
- derive and recall sums and differences of multiples of 10.
- derive and recall number pairs that total 100.
- identify the doubles of two-digit numbers and derive the corresponding halves.
- subtract mentally pairs of two-digit whole numbers.

Learning objectives

Objective 1: Use mental methods for subtracting whole numbers.

Learning outcomes

The children will be able to:
- use mental methods for an increasing range of subtractions.

Success criteria

The children have a **secure** level of attainment in relation to Objective 1 if the following question can be answered with a 'yes'.

Can the children...
... respond quickly and accurately to the questions?

Administering the assessment

Ensure that the children understand the task. Watch them carefully to see whether they have appropriate strategies for the calculations. Simple jottings should be allowed but this assessment is focused on mental methods and children should not use formal written methods. You can simply let the children work through the sheet at their own pace but you may prefer to dictate the questions below and limit the time allowed for each question to ten seconds. (The answers are provided after each question.)

Question 1: 60 minus 38	22
Question 2: 90 minus 47	43
Question 3: 80 minus 16	64
Question 4: 52 minus 14	38
Question 5: 73 minus 15	58
Question 6: 81 minus 16	65
Question 7: 92 minus 18	74
Question 8: 100 minus 59	41
Question 9: 100 minus 82	18
Question 10: 102 minus 13	89
Question 11: 106 minus 29	77
Question 12: 110 minus 45	65
Question 13: 208 minus 167	41
Question 14: 306 minus 128	178
Question 15: 401 minus 299	102
Question 16: 503 minus 196	307
Question 17: 810 minus 499	311
Question 18: 6004 minus 4999	1005
Question 19: 8060 minus 3992	4068
Question 20: 9014 minus 2991	6023

(This assessment will also provide evidence for assessing strand 1, Using and applying mathematics: Solve one-step and two-step problems involving whole numbers and fractions, choosing and using appropriate calculation strategies.)

Andrew Brodie: Ten Minute Maths Assessments ages 9–10 © A&C Black 2009

Extend mental methods for whole-number calculations (subtraction)

Name

Date

Write the answers in the correct boxes.

1. 60 - 38 =

2. 90 - 47 =

3. 80 - 16 =

4. 52 - 14 =

5. 73 - 15 =

6. 81 - 16 =

7. 92 - 18 =

8. 100 - 59 =

9. 100 - 82 =

10. 102 - 13 =

11. 106 - 29 =

12. 110 - 45 =

13. 208 - 167 =

14. 306 - 128 =

15. 401 - 299 =

16. 503 - 196 =

17. 810 - 499 =

18. 6004 - 4999 =

19. 8060 - 3992 =

20. 9014 - 2991 =

I can subtract numbers mentally.

Extend mental methods for whole-number calculations (multiplication)

Building on previous learning

Before starting this unit check that the children can already:
- recall quickly multiplication facts up to 10 x 10 and derive the corresponding division facts.
- multiply numbers to 1000 by 10 or 100.

Learning objectives

Objective 1: Use mental methods for multiplying whole numbers.

Learning outcomes

The children will be able to:
- use mental methods for an increasing range of multiplications.

Success criteria

The children have a **secure** level of attainment in relation to Objective 1 if the following question can be answered with a 'yes'.

Can the children...
... respond quickly and accurately to the questions?

Administering the assessment

Ensure that the children understand the task. Watch them carefully to see whether they have appropriate strategies for the calculations. Simple jottings should be allowed but this assessment focuses on mental methods so children should not use formal written methods. You can simply let the children work through the sheet at their own pace but you may prefer to dictate the questions below and limit the time allowed for each question to ten seconds.

Question 1: 12 times 9	*108*
Question 2: 14 times 4	*56*
Question 3: 17 times 3	*51*
Question 4: 19 times 5	*95*
Question 5: 12 times 7	*84*
Question 6: 16 times 6	*96*
Question 7: 18 times 7	*126*
Question 8: 19 times 6	*114*
Question 9: 13 times 5	*65*
Question 10: 15 times 5	*75*
Question 11: 16 times 4	*64*
Question 12: 17 times 4	*68*
Question 13: 14 times 9	*126*
Question 14: 16 times 9	*144*
Question 15: 18 times 8	*144*
Question 16: 12 times 12	*144*
Question 17: 24 times 6	*144*
Question 18: 16 times 25	*400*
Question 19: 9 times 25	*225*
Question 20: 20 times 25	*500*

(This assessment will also provide evidence for assessing strand 1, Using and applying mathematics: Solve one-step and two-step problems involving whole numbers and fractions, choosing and using appropriate calculation strategies.)

Andrew Brodie: Ten Minute Maths Assessments ages 9–10 © A&C Black 2009

Extend mental methods for whole-number calculations (multiplication)

Name

Date

Write the answers in the correct boxes.

1. 12 x 9 =

2. 14 x 4 =

3. 17 x 3 =

4. 19 x 5 =

5. 12 x 7 =

6. 16 x 6 =

7. 18 x 7 =

8. 19 x 6 =

9. 13 x 5 =

10. 15 x 5 =

11. 16 x 4 =

12. 17 x 4 =

13. 14 x 9 =

14. 16 x 9 =

15. 18 x 8 =

16. 12 x 12 =

17. 24 x 6 =

18. 16 x 25 =

19. 9 x 25 =

20. 20 x 25 =

I can multiply numbers mentally.

Andrew Brodie: Ten Minute Maths Assessments ages 9–10 © A&C Black 2009

Extend mental methods for whole-number calculations (division)

Building on previous learning

Before starting this unit check that the children can already:

- recall quickly multiplication facts up to 10 x 10 and derive the corresponding division facts.
- multiply and divide numbers to 1000 by 10 or 100.

Learning objectives

Objective 1: Use mental methods for dividing whole numbers.

Learning outcomes

The children will be able to:

- use mental methods for an increasing range of divisions.

Success criteria

The children have a **secure** level of attainment in relation to Objective 1 if the following question can be answered with a 'yes'.

Can the children…
… respond quickly and accurately to the questions?

Administering the assessment

Ensure that the children understand the task. Watch them carefully to see whether they have appropriate strategies for the calculations. Simple jottings should be allowed but this assessment focuses on mental methods so children should not use formal written methods. You can simply let the children work through the sheet at their own pace but you may prefer to dictate the questions below and limit the time allowed for each question to ten seconds.
(The answers are provided after each question.)

Question 1: 84 divided by 7	12
Question 2: 65 divided by 13	5
Question 3: 42 divided by 3	14
Question 4: 51 divided by 3	17
Question 5: 44 divided by 2	22
Question 6: 64 divided by 4	16
Question 7: 70 divided by 5	14
Question 8: 90 divided by 6	15
Question 9: 48 divided by 3	16
Question 10: 32 divided by 2	16
Question 11: 52 divided by 4	13
Question 12: 60 divided by 4	15
Question 13: 60 divided by 12	5
Question 14: 72 divided by 18	4
Question 15: 75 divided by 3	25
Question 16: 150 divided by 25	6
Question 17: 300 divided by 50	6
Question 18: 400 divided by 25	16
Question 19: 630 divided by 70	9
Question 20: 720 divided by 9	80

(This assessment will also provide evidence for assessing strand 1, Using and applying mathematics: Solve one-step and two-step problems involving whole numbers and fractions, choosing and using appropriate calculation strategies.)

Andrew Brodie: Ten Minute Maths Assessments ages 9–10 © A&C Black 2009

Extend mental methods for whole-number calculations (division)

Name

Date

Write the answers in the correct boxes.

1. 84 ÷ 7 =

2. 65 ÷ 13 =

3. 42 ÷ 3 =

4. 51 ÷ 3 =

5. 44 ÷ 2 =

6. 64 ÷ 4 =

7. 70 ÷ 5 =

8. 90 ÷ 6 =

9. 48 ÷ 3 =

10. 32 ÷ 2 =

11. 52 ÷ 4 =

12. 60 ÷ 4 =

13. 60 ÷ 12 =

14. 72 ÷ 18 =

15. 75 ÷ 3 =

16. 150 ÷ 25 =

17. 300 ÷ 50 =

18. 400 ÷ 25 =

19. 630 ÷ 70 =

20. 720 ÷ 9 =

I can divide numbers mentally.

Use efficient written methods to add whole numbers and decimals with up to two places

Building on previous learning

Before starting this unit check that the children can already:

- derive and recall all addition facts for each number to 20.
- derive and recall sums and differences of multiples of 10.
- derive and recall number pairs that total 100.
- identify the doubles of two-digit numbers and derive the corresponding halves.
- develop and use written methods to record, support or explain addition of two-digit and three-digit numbers.
- use mental methods for adding whole numbers.

Learning objectives

Objective 1: Use efficient written methods to add whole numbers and decimals with up to two places.

Learning outcomes

The children will be able to:

- use their own efficient written strategies to add whole numbers and decimals with up to two places.

Success criteria

The children have a **secure** level of attainment in relation to Objective 1 if the following question can be answered with a 'yes'.

Can the children...
... complete the assessment questions confidently and quickly by using an appropriate strategy for addition?

Administering the assessment

Discuss the layout of the assessment sheet with the pupils, pointing out that space is provided for working out the answers. The assessment focuses on whether the pupils have an appropriate written strategy for addition of whole numbers and decimals. Each child's strategy may be a method that they have been shown in school or at home but this assessment is concerned with the requirement to use an 'efficient' written method. You may need to refer to your school policy on calculation, which will specify an appropriate method.

The final question is an extension activity as it puts the operation in the context of a problem. Some children will need help with reading the question.

(This assessment will also provide evidence for assessing strand 1, Using and applying mathematics: Solve one-step and two-step problems involving whole numbers and decimals; Represent a puzzle or problem by identifying and recording the information or calculations needed to solve it; find possible solutions and confirm them in the context of the problem.)

Answers: *27.85*   *30.19*   *46.1*   *8.26m*

Use efficient written methods to add whole numbers and decimals with up to two places

Name

Date

Use the working out space to help you answer each addition question.

23.6 + 4.25

Answer

7.2 + 19 + 3.99

Answer

5.75 + 28.1 + 12.25

Answer

One plank is 4.37 metres long and the other is 3.89 metres long. What is the total length of the two pieces of wood?

Answer

I can use written methods for the addition of whole numbers and decimals.

Use efficient written methods to subtract whole numbers and decimals with up to two places

Building on previous learning

Before starting this unit check that the children can already:

- derive and recall all subtraction facts for each number to 20.
- derive and recall sums and differences of multiples of 10.
- derive and recall number pairs that total 100.
- identify the doubles of two-digit numbers and derive the corresponding halves.
- develop and use written methods to record, support or explain subtraction of two-digit and three-digit numbers.
- use mental methods for subtracting whole numbers.

Learning objectives

Objective 1: Use efficient written methods to subtract whole numbers and decimals with up to two places.

Learning outcomes

The children will be able to:

- use their own efficient written strategies to subtract whole numbers and decimals with up to two places.

Success criteria

The children have a **secure** level of attainment in relation to Objective 1 if the following question can be answered with a 'yes'.

Can the children…
… complete the assessment questions confidently and quickly by using an appropriate strategy for subtraction?

Administering the assessment

Discuss the layout of the assessment sheet with the pupils, pointing out that space is provided for working out the answers. The assessment focuses on whether the pupils have an appropriate written strategy for subtraction of whole numbers and decimals. Each child's strategy may be a method that they have been shown in school or at home but this assessment is concerned with the requirement to use an 'efficient' written method. You may need to refer to your school policy on calculation, which will specify an appropriate method.

The final question is an extension activity as it puts the operation in the context of a problem. Some children will need help with reading the question.

(This assessment will also provide evidence for assessing strand 1, Using and applying mathematics: Solve one-step and two-step problems involving whole numbers and decimals; Represent a puzzle or problem by identifying and recording the information or calculations needed to solve it; find possible solutions and confirm them in the context of the problem.)

Answers: *8.25*   *3.7*   *14.53*   *2.55m*

Use efficient written methods to subtract whole numbers and decimals with up to two places

Name

Date

Use the working out space to help you answer each subtraction question.

12 − 3.75

Answer

6.1 − 2.4

Answer

27.03 − 12.5

Answer

A plank of wood is 4.3 metres long. If 1.75 metres are cut off, what is the length of the piece that is left?

Answer

I can use written methods for the subtraction of whole numbers and decimals.

Multiply whole numbers and decimals by 10, 100 or 1000

Building on previous learning

Before starting this unit check that the children can already:

- recognise multiples of 10 up to 1000.
- recall multiplication facts for the 10 times table.

Learning objectives

Objective 1: Use understanding of place value to multiply whole numbers and decimals by 10, 100 or 1000.

Learning outcomes

The children will be able to:

- multiply whole numbers and decimals by 10, 100 or 1000.

Success criteria

The children have a **secure** level of attainment in relation to Objective 1 if the following question can be answered with a 'yes'.

Can the children...

... complete the assessment questions confidently and quickly?

Administering the assessment

Before starting the written part of the assessment discuss some questions with the children e.g. 326 x 10 and 48 x 100. Can each child explain what is happening? Do not accept 'adding a zero' or 'adding two zeroes' – this is not what is happening. Instead the child should be able to explain the process in relation to place value. Now ask the children questions such as 4.8 x 10, 3.6 x 100 and 6.2 x 1000. Again, the children should be able to use their knowledge of place value to write the correct answers with each digit in the appropriate 'column'. Make sure that the children understand how they are to show their answers on the assessment sheet. You can simply let the children work through the sheet at their own pace but you may prefer to dictate the questions below and limit the time allowed for each question to five seconds.

(The answers are provided after each question.)

Question 1:	10 times 82	820
Question 2:	10 times 295	2950
Question 3:	416 times 10	4160
Question 4:	62 times 100	6200
Question 5:	14 times 1000	14000
Question 6:	100 times 38	3800
Question 7:	1000 times 49	49000
Question 8:	6.4 times 10	64
Question 9:	10 times 3.9	39
Question 10:	10 times 0.7	7
Question 11:	100 times 1.2	120
Question 12:	4.7 times 100	470
Question 13:	6.25 times 100	625
Question 14:	100 times 62.5	6250
Question 15:	47.3 times 100	4730
Question 16:	13.05 times 100	1305
Question 17:	9.2 times 1000	9200
Question 18:	2.35 times 1000	2350
Question 19:	1000 times 0.8	800
Question 20:	0.02 times 1000	20

(This assessment will also provide evidence for assessing strand 1, Using and applying mathematics: Explore patterns, properties and relationships and propose a general statement involving numbers or shapes; identify examples for which the statement is true or false; Solve one-step and two-step problems involving whole numbers and decimals.)

Multiply whole numbers and decimals by 10, 100 or 1000

Name

Date

Write the answers in the correct boxes.

1. 10 x 82 =

2. 10 x 295 =

3. 416 x 10 =

4. 62 x 100 =

5. 14 x 1000 =

6. 100 x 38 =

7. 1000 x 49 =

8. 6.4 x 10 =

9. 10 x 3.9 =

10. 10 x 0.7 =

11. 100 x 1.2 =

12. 4.7 x 100 =

13. 6.25 x 100 =

14. 100 x 62.5 =

15. 47.3 x 100 =

16. 13.05 x 100 =

17. 9.2 x 1000 =

18. 2.35 x 1000 =

19. 1000 x 0.8 =

20. 0.02 x 1000 =

I can multiply whole numbers and decimals by 10, 100 or 1000.

Divide whole numbers and decimals by 10, 100 or 1000

Building on previous learning

Before starting this unit check that the children can already:

- recognise multiples of 10 up to 1000.
- recall multiplication facts for the 10 times table and the corresponding division facts.

Learning objectives

Objective 1: Use understanding of place value to divide whole numbers and decimals by 10, 100 or 1000.

Learning outcomes

The children will be able to:

- divide whole numbers and decimals by 10, 100 or 1000.

Success criteria

The children have a **secure** level of attainment in relation to Objective 1 if the following question can be answered with a 'yes'.

Can the children…

… complete the assessment questions confidently and quickly?

Administering the assessment

Before starting the written part of the assessment discuss some questions with the children e.g. 400 ÷ 10. Can each child explain what is happening? 'Taking away a zero' is not acceptable as this is not what is happening. Instead the children should be able to explain the process in relation to place value. Now ask the children questions such as 5.6 ÷ 10 or 6.2 ÷ 100. Again, the children should be able to use their knowledge of place value to write the answers correctly with each digit in the appropriate 'column'. Ensure that the children understand how they should show their answers on the sheet. You can simply let the children work through the sheet at their own pace but you may prefer to dictate the questions below and limit the time allowed for each question to five seconds.
(The answers are provided after each question.)

Question 1: 920 divided by 10	92
Question 2: 830 divided by 10	83
Question 3: 765 divided by 10	76.5
Question 4: 382 divided by 10	38.2
Question 5: 69 divided by 10	6.9
Question 6: 76 divided by 10	7.6
Question 7: 48.4 divided by 10	4.84
Question 8: 7 divided by 10	0.7
Question 9: 4.2 divided by 10	0.42
Question 10: 0.3 divided by 10	0.03
Question 11: 0.25 divided by 10	0.025
Question 12: 469 divided by 100	4.69
Question 13: 328 divided by 100	3.28
Question 14: 86 divided by 100	0.86
Question 15: 75 divided by 100	0.75
Question 16: 9 divided by 100	0.09
Question 17: 6 divided by 100	0.06
Question 18: 684 divided by 1000	0.684
Question 19: 2642 divided by 1000	2.642
Question 20: 17500 divided by 1000	17.5

(This assessment will also provide evidence for assessing strand 1, Using and applying mathematics: Explore patterns, properties and relationships and propose a general statement involving numbers or shapes; identify examples for which the statement is true or false; Solve one-step and two-step problems involving whole numbers and decimals.)

Divide whole numbers and decimals by 10, 100 or 1000

Name

Date

Write the answers in the correct boxes.

1. $920 \div 10 =$

2. $830 \div 10 =$

3. $765 \div 10 =$

4. $382 \div 10 =$

5. $69 \div 10 =$

6. $76 \div 10 =$

7. $48.4 \div 10 =$

8. $7 \div 10 =$

9. $4.2 \div 10 =$

10. $0.3 \div 10 =$

11. $0.25 \div 10 =$

12. $469 \div 100 =$

13. $328 \div 100 =$

14. $86 \div 100 =$

15. $75 \div 100 =$

16. $9 \div 100 =$

17. $6 \div 100 =$

18. $684 \div 1000 =$

19. $2642 \div 1000 =$

20. $17500 \div 1000 =$

I can divide whole numbers and decimals by 10, 100 or 1000.

Refine and use efficient written methods to multiply HTU by units

Building on previous learning

Before starting this unit check that the children can already:

- recall multiplication facts up to 10 x 10.
- use written methods to record, support and explain multiplication of two-digit numbers by a one-digit number.

Learning objectives

Objective 1: Refine and use efficient written methods to multiply HTU by units.

Learning outcomes

The children will be able to:

- use appropriate strategies to multiply three-digit numbers by a one-digit number, in accordance with the school's calculation policy.

Success criteria

The children have a **secure** level of attainment in relation to Objective 1 if the following question can be answered with a 'yes'.

Can the children...

... complete the assessment questions confidently and quickly by using an appropriate strategy for multiplication?

Administering the assessment

Discuss the layout of the assessment sheet with the pupils, pointing out that space is provided for working out the answers. The assessment focuses on whether the pupils have an appropriate written strategy for multiplication of three-digit numbers by one-digit numbers. You should refer to your school policy on calculation, which will specify an appropriate method. The final question is an extension activity as it puts the operation in the context of a problem. Some children will need help with reading the question.

(This assessment will also provide evidence for assessing strand 1, Using and applying mathematics: Solve one-step and two-step problems involving whole numbers and decimals; Represent a puzzle or problem by identifying and recording the information or calculations needed to solve it; find possible solutions and confirm them in the context of the problem.)

Answers: *2790   7384   4613   £795*

Refine and use efficient written methods to multiply HTU by units

Name

Date

Use the working out space to help you answer each multiplication question.

465 x 6

Answer

923 x 8

Answer

659 x 7

Answer

A television costs £265.
How much will 3 of these
televisions cost altogether?

Answer

I can multiply three-digit numbers by a one-digit number.

Refine and use efficient written methods to multiply TU by TU

Building on previous learning

Before starting this unit check that the children can already:

- recall multiplication facts up to 10 x 10.
- use written methods to record, support and explain multiplication of two-digit numbers by a one-digit number.
- use efficient written methods to multiply HTU by U.

Learning objectives

Objective 1: Refine and use efficient written methods to multiply TU by TU.

Learning outcomes

The children will be able to:

- use appropriate strategies to multiply a two-digit whole number by another two-digit whole number, in accordance with the school's calculation policy.

Success criteria

The children have a **secure** level of attainment in relation to Objective 1 if the following question can be answered with a 'yes'.

Can the children…

… complete the assessment questions confidently and quickly by using an appropriate strategy for multiplication?

Administering the assessment

Discuss the layout of the assessment sheet with the pupils, pointing out that space is provided for working out the answers. The assessment focuses on whether the pupils have an appropriate written strategy for multiplication of two-digit numbers by other two-digit numbers. You should refer to your school policy on calculation, which will specify an appropriate method. The final question is an extension activity as it puts the operation in the context of a problem. Some children will need help with reading the question.

(This assessment will also provide evidence for assessing strand 1, Using and applying mathematics: Solve one-step and two-step problems involving whole numbers and decimals; Represent a puzzle or problem by identifying and recording the information or calculations needed to solve it; find possible solutions and confirm them in the context of the problem.)

Answers: *476*   *3528*   *625*   *736 chocolate buttons*

Refine and use efficient written methods to multiply TU by TU

Name

Date

Use the working out space to help you answer each multiplication question.

28 x 17

Answer

98 x 36

Answer

25 x 25

Answer

There are 23 chocolate buttons in a packet.
How many chocolate buttons are there altogether in 32 packets?

Answer

I can multiply two-digit numbers by two-digit numbers.

Refine and use efficient written methods to multiply U.t by U

Building on previous learning

Before starting this unit check that the children can already:
- recall multiplication facts up to 10 x 10.
- use written methods to record, support and explain multiplication of two-digit numbers by a one-digit number.
- use efficient written methods to multiply HTU by U.

Learning objectives

Objective 1: Refine and use efficient written methods to multiply U.t x U.

Learning outcomes

The children will be able to:
- use appropriate strategies to multiply a two-digit number consisting of a units digit and a tenths digit by a single digit whole number, in accordance with the school's calculation policy.

Success criteria

The children have a **secure** level of attainment in relation to Objective 1 if the following question can be answered with a 'yes'.

Can the children...
... complete the assessment questions confidently and quickly by using an appropriate strategy for multiplication?

Administering the assessment

Discuss the layout of the assessment sheet with the pupils, pointing out that space is provided for working out the answers. The assessment focuses on whether the pupils have an appropriate written strategy for multiplying a two-digit number consisting of a units digit and a tenths digit by a single digit whole number. You should refer to your school policy on calculation, which will specify an appropriate method. The final question is an extension activity as it puts the operation in the context of a problem. Some children will need help with reading the question.

(This assessment will also provide evidence for assessing strand 1, Using and applying mathematics: Solve one-step and two-step problems involving whole numbers and decimals; Represent a puzzle or problem by identifying and recording the information or calculations needed to solve it; find possible solutions and confirm them in the context of the problem.)

Answers: 13.3   27.2   50.4   12.6m

Refine and use efficient written methods to multiply U.t x U

Name

Date

Use the working out space to help you answer each multiplication question.

1.9 x 7

Answer

3.4 x 8

Answer

5.6 x 9

Answer

A skipping rope is 1.8 metres long. If seven of these skipping ropes were laid end to end what length would they reach altogether?

Answer

I can multiply units and tenths by units.

Andrew Brodie: Ten Minute Maths Assessments ages 9–10 © A&C Black 2009

Refine and use efficient written methods to divide HTU by U

Building on previous learning

Before starting this unit check that the children can already:

- recall multiplication facts up to 10 x 10 and the corresponding division facts.
- use written methods to record, support and explain division of two-digit numbers by a one-digit number.

Learning objectives

Objective 1: Refine and use efficient written methods to divide HTU ÷ U.

Learning outcomes

The children will be able to:

- use appropriate strategies to divide three-digit numbers by a one-digit number, in accordance with the school's calculation policy.

Success criteria

The children have a **secure** level of attainment in relation to Objective 1 if the following question can be answered with a 'yes'.

Can the children…

… complete the assessment questions confidently and quickly by using an appropriate strategy for division?

Administering the assessment

Discuss the layout of the assessment sheet with the pupils, pointing out that space is provided for working out the answers. The assessment focuses on whether the pupils have an appropriate written strategy for division of three-digit numbers by one-digit numbers. You should refer to your school policy on calculation, which will specify an appropriate method. The final question is an extension activity as it puts the operation in the context of a problem. Some children will need help with reading the question.

(This assessment will also provide evidence for assessing strand 1, Using and applying mathematics: Solve one-step and two-step problems involving whole numbers and decimals; Represent a puzzle or problem by identifying and recording the information or calculations needed to solve it; find possible solutions and confirm them in the context of the problem.)

Answers: 89   138   235   129

Refine and use efficient written methods to divide HTU by U

Name

Date

Use the working out space to help you answer each division question.

267 ÷ 3

Answer

966 ÷ 7

Answer

940 ÷ 4

Answer

There are 516 children in a school. The children are to be split into four equal sized groups.
How many children will be in each group?

Answer

I can divide three-digit numbers by a one-digit number.

Find fractions of numbers and quantities using division

Building on previous learning

Before starting this unit check that the children can already:
- derive and recall multiplication facts up to 10 x 10, and the corresponding division facts.
- read and write proper fractions.
- find fractions of numbers, quantities or shapes.

Learning objectives

Objective 1: Find fractions of numbers and quantities using division.

Learning outcomes

The children will be able to:
- find fractions of numbers (e.g. $\frac{1}{8}$ of 96) and of quantities (e.g. $\frac{1}{10}$ of 5 metres).

Success criteria

The children have a **secure** level of attainment in relation to Objective 1 if the following question can be answered with a 'yes'.

Can the children...

... complete the assessment questions confidently and quickly?

Administering the assessment

Make sure the children understand how to show their answers on the assessment sheet. Discuss the following question, explaining that the answer could be given with two different units: What is $\frac{1}{10}$ of 5 metres? The answer could be given as 0.5 m or as 50 cm. Both of these answers are correct and either is acceptable. Encourage the pupils to be aware of the appropriate units when answering questions relating to quantities. You can simply let the children work through the sheet at their own pace but you may prefer to dictate the questions below and limit the time allowed for each question to ten seconds. (The answers are provided after each question.)

Question 1: What is one third of 36?	*12*
Question 2: What is one quarter of 120?	*30*
Question 3: What is one fifth of 400?	*80*
Question 4: What is one eighth of 96?	*12*
Question 5: What is one seventh of 98?	*14*
Question 6: What is one sixth of 90?	*15*
Question 7: What is one ninth of 144?	*16*
Question 8: What is one tenth of 4 metres?	*0.4m or 40cm*
Question 9: What is one hundredth of 5 kilograms?	*0.05kg or 50g*
Question 10: What is one tenth of 8 litres?	*0.8l or 800ml*
Question 11: What is one quarter of 6 metres?	*1.5 m*
Question 12: What is three quarters of 3 metres?	*2.25m*

(This assessment will also provide evidence for assessing strand 1, Using and applying mathematics: Solve one-step and two-step problems involving whole numbers and decimals; Represent a puzzle or problem by identifying and recording the information or calculations needed to solve it; find possible solutions and confirm them in the context of the problem.)

Find fractions of numbers and quantities using division

Name

Date

Write the answers in the correct boxes.

1. What is one third of 36?

2. What is one quarter of 120?

3. What is one fifth of 400?

4. What is one eighth of 96?

5. What is one seventh of 98?

6. What is one sixth of 90?

7. What is one ninth of 144?

8. What is one tenth of 4 m?

9. What is one hundreth of 5 kg?

10. What is one tenth of 8 litres?

11. What is one quarter of 6 m?

12. What is three quarters of 3 m?

I can use division to find fractions of numbers and quantities.

Andrew Brodie: Ten Minute Maths Assessments ages 9–10 © A&C Black 2009

Find percentages of numbers and quantities

Building on previous learning

Before starting this unit check that the children can already:

- derive and recall multiplication facts up to 10 x 10, and the corresponding division facts.
- use understanding of place value to divide whole numbers and decimals by 10.
- use mental methods for multiplying whole numbers.

Learning objectives

Objective 1: Find percentages of numbers and quantities.

Learning outcomes

The children will be able to:

- find common percentages (10%, 50%, 25%, 5%, 15%) of numbers and quantities.

Success criteria

The children have a **secure** level of attainment in relation to Objective 1 if the following question can be answered with a 'yes'.

Can the children...

... complete the assessment questions confidently and quickly?

Administering the assessment

Ensure that the children understand how to show their answers on the assessment sheet. This assessment focuses on whether pupils are aware that percentages can be calculated in relation to common fractions e.g. 50% is equivalent to $\frac{1}{2}$; 25% is equivalent to $\frac{1}{4}$; 10% is equivalent to $\frac{1}{10}$. They can make use of these facts to find other percentages e.g. 5% is half of 10%, 15% is 10% and 5% combined, etc. You can simply let the children work through the sheet at their own pace but you may prefer to dictate the questions below and limit the time allowed for each question to ten seconds.

(The answers are provided after each question.)

Question 1: What is 50% of 120?	60
Question 2: What is 50% of 700?	350
Question 3: What is 25% of 20?	5
Question 4: What is 25% of 60?	15
Question 5: What is 10% of 200?	20
Question 6: What is 20% of 200?	40
Question 7: What is 10% of 300?	30
Question 8: What is 30% of 300?	90
Question 9: What is 40% of £60?	£24
Question 10: What is 70% of £90?	£63
Question 11: What is 5% of £80?	£4
Question 12: What is 15% of £80?	£12

(This assessment will also provide evidence for assessing strand 1, Using and applying mathematics: Solve one-step and two-step problems involving whole numbers and decimals; Represent a puzzle or problem by identifying and recording the information or calculations needed to solve it; find possible solutions and confirm them in the context of the problem.)

Find percentages of numbers and quantities

Name

Date

Write the answers in the correct boxes.

1. What is 50% of 120?

2. What is 50% of 700?

3. What is 25% of 20?

4. What is 25% of 60?

5. What is 10% of 200?

6. What is 20% of 200?

7. What is 10% of 300?

8. What is 30% of 300?

9. What is 40% of £60?

10. What is 70% of £90?

11. What is 5% of £80?

12. What is 15% of £80?

I can find percentages of numbers and quantities.

Andrew Brodie: Ten Minute Maths Assessments ages 9–10 © A&C Black 2009

Use a calculator to solve problems

Building on previous learning

Before starting this unit check that the children can already:
- use knowledge of rounding, number operations and inverses to estimate and check calculations.

Learning objectives

Objective 1: Use a calculator to solve problems, including those involving decimals or fractions.

Learning outcomes

The children will be able to:
- use a calculator to solve problems, including those involving decimals or fractions; interpret the display correctly in the context of measurement.

Success criteria

The children have a **secure** level of attainment in relation to Objective 1 if the following questions can be answered with a 'yes'.

Can the children...
... complete the assessment questions confidently and quickly?
... convert the units appropriately in questions 4 and 5?
... write the amounts of money correctly in questions 7, 8, 10 and 12?

Administering the assessment

Ensure that the children understand how to show their answers on the assessment sheet. Note that questions 4 and 5 can be used to gain evidence of pupils' ability to 'convert larger to smaller units using decimals to one place'. This assessment can also be used to assess how pupils use knowledge of rounding, place value, number facts and inverse operations to estimate and check calculations. You can simply let the children work through the sheet at their own pace but you may prefer to dictate the questions below and limit the time allowed for each question to ten seconds.
(The answers are provided after each question.)

Question 1: What is the total of 2453, 318 and 92.7?   2863.7
Question 2: What is the difference between 9148 and 3654?   5494
Question 3: What is half of 6193?   3096.5
Question 4: What is the total of 1.5 kilograms and 620 grams. Give your answer in grams.   2120g
Question 5: A piece of wood is 2.6 metres long. Another piece of wood is 45 centimetres long. What is the total length of the two pieces of wood when they are placed end to end? Give your answer in centimetres.   305cm
Question 6: Find three quarters of 300 metres.   225m
Question 7: £96.40 is shared between 8 people. How much money do they have each?   £12.05
Question 8: £237 is shared between 6 people. How much money do they have each?   £39.50
Question 9: What is the product of 425 and 86?   36550
Question 10: What is £163.10 divided by 7?   £23.30
Question 11: What is the product of 0.5 and 0.4?   0.2
Question 12: I spend £26.49 and £18.62. What is my change from £100?   £54.89

(This assessment will also provide evidence for assessing strand 1, Using and applying mathematics: Solve one-step and two-step problems involving whole numbers and decimals and all four operations, choosing and using appropriate calculation strategies, including calculator use; Represent a puzzle or problem by identifying and recording the information or calculations needed to solve it; find possible solutions and confirm them in the context of the problem.)

Use a calculator to solve problems

Name

Date

Use a calculator to answer these questions.
Write the answers in the correct boxes.

1. What is the total of 2453, 318 and 92.7?

2. What is the difference between 9148 and 3654?

3. What is half of 6193?

4. What is the total of 1.5kg and 620g?

5. What is the total length of 2.6 metres and 45cm?

6. Find three quarters of 300 metres?

7. £96.40 is shared between 8 people. How much money do they have each?

8. £237 is shared between 6 people. How much money do they have each?

9. What is the product of 425 and 86?

10. What is £613.10 divided by 7?

11. What is the product of 0.5 and 0.4?

12. I spend £26.49 and £18.62. What is my change from £100?

I can use a calculator to solve problems.

I can convert larger to smaller units using decimals to one place.

Read and plot coordinates in the first quadrant

Building on previous learning

Before starting this unit check that the children can already:

- follow and give instructions involving position, direction and movement.
- read and record the vocabulary of position, direction and movement, using the four compass directions to describe movement about a grid.

Learning objectives

Objective 1: Read and plot coordinates in the first quadrant.

Learning outcomes

The children will be able to:

- read coordinates in the first quadrant.
- plot coordinates in the first quadrant.

Success criteria

The children have a **secure** level of attainment in relation to Objective 1 if the following questions can be answered with a 'yes'.

Can the children…

- … identify the position of any point on the grid by using coordinates, giving the *x* value before the *y* value?
- … write the coordinates correctly, within brackets and separated by commas?
- … identify the coordinates of points A, B, C and D?
- … plot the coordinates for E, F, G and H?

Administering the assessment

Ensure that the children can read the words on the assessment sheet. Many children are familiar with the mnemonic 'along the corridor and up the stairs' to help them to remember that they must give the coordinate in the *x* direction before the coordinate in the *y* direction.

(This assessment will also provide evidence for assessing strand 1, Using and applying mathematics: Explain reasoning using diagrams, graphs and text; refine ways of recording using images and symbols.)

Answers: A (2, 7)   B (4, 2)   C (9, 4)   D (7, 9)

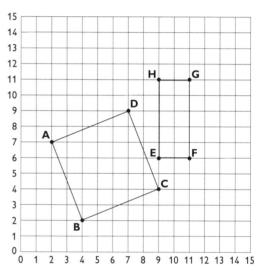

Read and plot coordinates in the first quadrant

Name

Date

Look at the grid.
Four points A, B, C and D are marked on the grid.
Join these points to make a square.

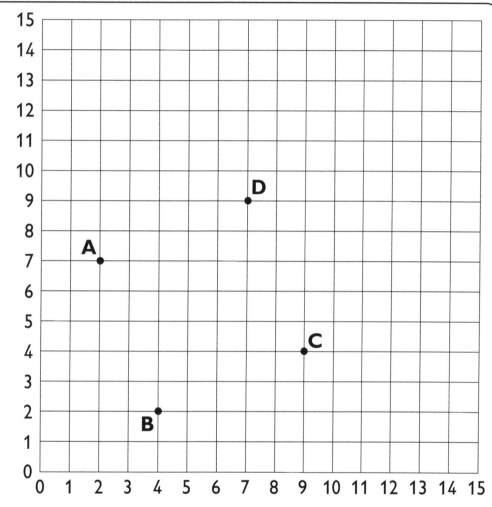

Give the coordinates for the four points:

A marks the point   ------------------

B marks the point   ------------------

C marks the point   ------------------

D marks the point   ------------------

Now draw a rectangle on the grid with the following coordinates for its corners:

E should mark the point (9, 6)
F should mark the point (11, 6)
G should mark the point (11, 11)
H should mark the point (9, 11)

I can read coordinates in the first quadrant. ☐

I can plot coordinates in the first quadrant. ☐

Complete patterns with up to two lines of symmetry; draw the position of a shape after a reflection

Building on previous learning

Before starting this unit check that the children can already:

- describe, visualise, classify and draw 2-D shapes.
- sort, make and describe shapes, referring to their properties.
- identify reflective symmetry in patterns.
- identify reflective symmetry in 2-D shapes and draw lines of symmetry in shapes.

Learning objectives

Objective 1: Complete patterns with up to 2 lines of symmetry.

Objective 2: Draw the position of a shape after a reflection.

Learning outcomes

The children will be able to:

- reflect a shape twice to produce a symmetrical pattern with two lines of symmetry.
- draw the reflection of a shape in a specified line.

Success criteria

The children have a **secure** level of attainment in relation to Objective 1 if the following questions can be answered with a 'yes'.

Can the children…

… draw the reflection of the pentagon in line A then the reflection of the original pentagon and its image in line B?

… draw the reflection of the rectangle in line A?

Administering the assessment

Ensure that the children can read the words on the assessment sheet and that they recognise the shape on the sheet as a pentagon as it has five sides. You could ask them to explain why it is not a regular pentagon.

(This assessment will also provide evidence for assessing strand 1, Using and applying mathematics: Explain reasoning using diagrams, graphs and text; refine ways of recording using images and symbols; Explore patterns, properties and relationships and propose a general statement involving numbers or shapes; identify examples for which the statement is true or false.)

Answers:

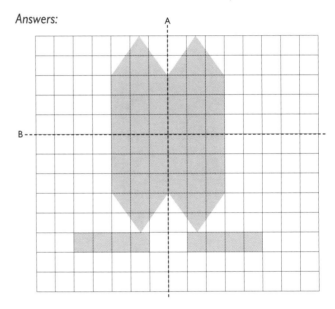

Andrew Brodie: Ten Minute Maths Assessments ages 9–10 © A&C Black 2009

Complete patterns with up to two lines of symmetry

Name

Date

Look at the grid. Two mirror lines are marked A and B.
Draw the reflection of the pentagon in line A.
Now draw the reflection of the two pentagons in line B.

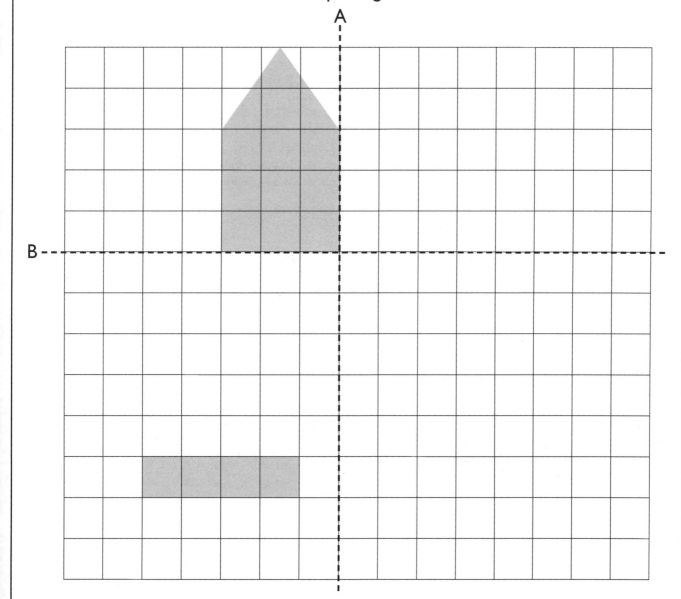

Now draw the reflection of the rectangle in line A.

I can complete patterns with up to two lines of symmetry.

I can draw the position of a shape after a reflection.

Estimate, draw and measure acute and obtuse angles using an angle measurer or protractor to a suitable degree of accuracy; calculate angles in a straight line

Building on previous learning

Before starting this unit check that the children can already:
- use a set-square to draw right angles.
- identify right angles in 2-D shapes.
- compare angles with a right angle.
- compare and order angles less than 180°.
- know that angles are measured in degrees and that one whole turn is 360°.

Learning objectives

Objective 1: Estimate and measure acute and obtuse angles using an angle measurer or protractor to a suitable degree of accuracy.

Learning outcomes

The children will be able to:
- estimate and measure acute and obtuse angles using an angle measurer or protractor to a suitable degree of accuracy.
- draw lines at specified angles.
- calculate angles in a straight line.

Success criteria

The children have a **secure** level of attainment in relation to Objective 1 if the following questions can be answered with a 'yes'.

Can the children…
… state whether each angle is acute or obtuse?
… make effective assessments of the angles shown?
… measure the angles accurately?

Administering the assessment

Ensure that the children understand the tasks. Watch carefully how they use the protractor or angle measurer – many children make errors because they do not understand the calibration on the protractor. Once they have completed the worksheet ask them to draw some lines at angles that you specify e.g. 30°, 129°, 75°, 100°. Now return to the assessment sheet and extend one of the lines for each angle. Can the children work out what the new angle is? (180° minus the angle that they have already measured.)

(This assessment will also provide evidence for assessing strand 1, Using and applying mathematics: Explain reasoning using diagrams, graphs and text; refine ways of recording using images and symbols; Explore patterns, properties and relationships and propose a general statement involving numbers or shapes; identify examples for which the statement is true or false.)

Answers: A 123°   B 60°   C 45°   D 160°

Estimate, draw and measure acute and obtuse angles

Name

Date

Look at the angles. Label each angle with 'acute' or 'obtuse'.

A

B
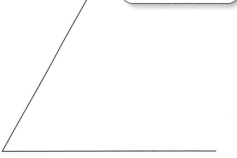

C
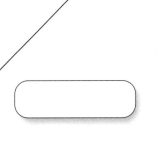

D

Now make an estimate of the size of each angle.

Angle A is approximately ....

Angle B is approximately ....

Angle C is approximately ....

Angle D is approximately ....

Now measure the size of each angle.

Angle A = ...

Angle B = ...

Angle C = ...

Angle D = ...

I can estimate acute and obtuse angles.

I can measure acute and obtuse angles.

I can draw acute and obtuse angles.

Draw and measure lines to the nearest millimetre; measure and calculate the perimeter of regular and irregular polygons

Building on previous learning

Before starting this unit check that the children can already:
- describe, visualise, classify and draw 2-D shapes.
- sort, make and describe shapes, referring to their properties.
- draw rectangles and measure and calculate their perimeters.

Learning objectives

Objective 1: Measure lines to the nearest millimetre.
Objective 2: Draw lines to the nearest millimetre.
Objective 3: Measure and calculate the perimeter of regular and irregular polygons.

Learning outcomes

The children will be able to:
- measure lines to the nearest millimetre.
- calculate the perimeters of 2-D shapes by adding the lengths of the sides.
- use appropriate units of millimetres or centimetres.

Success criteria

The children have a **secure** level of attainment in relation to Objective 1 if the following questions can be answered with a 'yes'.

Can the children...
... measure accurately the lengths of the sides of the shapes shown?
... add the lengths of sides together to find the perimeters?
... draw lines of specified lengths?

Administering the assessment

Ensure that the pupils can read the instructions on the assessment sheet. Watch how the pupils use their rulers, ensuring that they start measuring from the 0 mark rather than from the 1 or from the very end of the ruler. Once the pupils have completed the assessment sheet, assess their ability to draw lines accurately by asking them to draw lines of specified lengths on the back of the sheet e.g. 72mm, 125mm, 8.9cm, 5.7cm

(This assessment will also provide evidence for assessing strand 1, Using and applying mathematics: Solve one-step and two-step problems involving whole numbers and decimals, choosing and using appropriate calculation strategies; Explore patterns, properties and relationships and propose a general statement involving numbers or shapes; identify examples for which the statement is true or false.)

Answers: *Perimeter of square = 212mm or 21.2cm*
             Perimeter of triangle = 222mm or 22.2cm
             Perimeter of pentagon = 220mm or 22cm

Draw and measure lines to the nearest millimetre; measure and calculate the perimeter of regular and irregular polygons

Name

Date

Measure the lengths of each side of the shapes shown.
Use your measurements to calculate the perimeter of the shapes.

Square

Perimeter in millimetres = _____

Perimeter in centimetres = _____

Scalene triangle

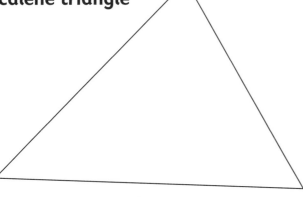

Pentagon

Perimeter in millimetres = _____

Perimeter in centimetres = _____

Perimeter in millimetres = _____

Perimeter in centimetres = _____

I can measure lines to the nearest millimetre.

I can measure and calculate the perimeter of regular and irregular polygons.

Andrew Brodie: Ten Minute Maths Assessments ages 9–10 © A&C Black 2009

Squared paper

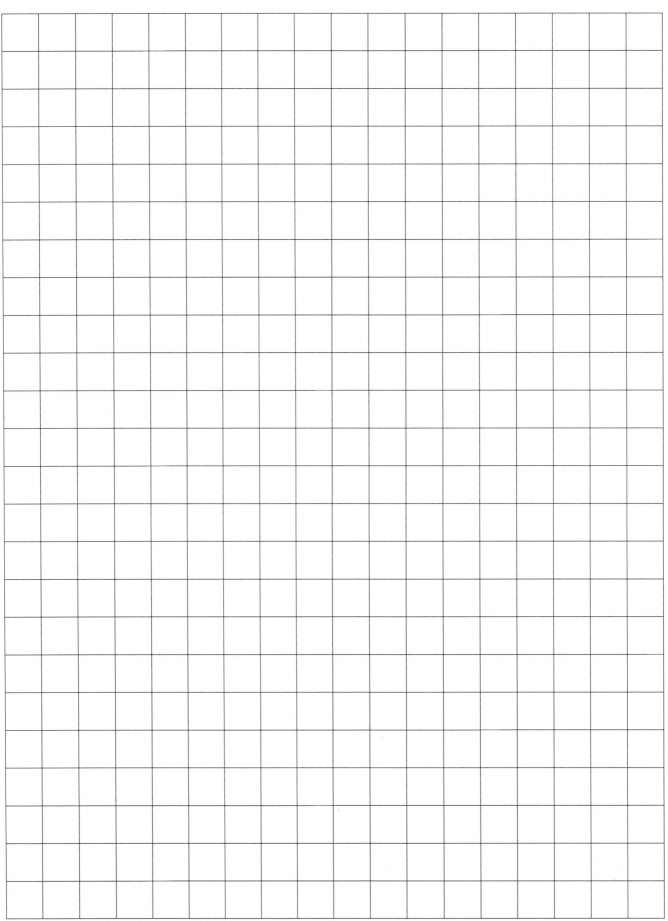

Andrew Brodie: Ten Minute Maths Assessments ages 9–10 © A&C Black 2009